CW00435569

All Who Sail in Us

by

Cecily Holland

Copyright © 2019 Cecily Holland

All rights reserved. No part of this publication may be reproduced, stored in or introduced into a retrieval system, or transmitted in any form or by any means (electronic, recording or otherwise), without the prior written permission of the above publisher of the book.

ISBN: 978-1-794-413429

To my darling Georgie

CONTENTS

Foreword

All Who Sail In Us is set in the spring of 1978 and follows the true story of Cecily, a 22-year-old working class lesbian, as she arrives to live in Stepney in the East End of London after hitchhiking down from the North of England. She is followed by her 18-year-old sister, also a lesbian, who are the 'only gays' in a massive family of eleven girls and two boys. The house in Stepney was one in a row of ten squats, five squatted by Asian families and the other five by lesbians, both communities looking out for each other. Full of passion, and despite Cecily's fragile broken heart, the two sisters managed to have the time of their lives with a plethora of women, partying, pool playing and spliffs that abounded. Life was tough with constant threats towards 'out' lesbians - a rare sight - as well as dodging IRA bombs, homophobes' bullets, police brutality, racists, fascists and being stranded in the Brixton riots. This was no place for the faint hearted, yet full of fun and thrilling all at the same time.

All Who Sail in Us

Full of East End Promise

Friday 3rd March 1978

I arrived at Aldgate East tube station at about 8 o'clock in the evening; it was dark on the unfamiliar streets of East London. None of the buses made any sense to me, I couldn't see any offering to take me where I wanted to go and they just sailed past me one after the other. Whitechapel Road, Aldgate, Commercial Street, Tubby Isaac's Takeaway kiosk, signs for the City, signs for the docks, where the hell is my street? There we are, at last I spotted Commercial Road. I hoisted me massive rucksack onto my back properly and set off walking. I couldn't be bothered to wait for a bus and wasn't sure where to get off anyway, so I carried myself and the dead weight of my rucksack the mile down Commercial Road to my new home in Wingate Street, Stepney, London E1.

Number 30 was my first stop, to pick up the key for my house which was number 42. There were ten terraced houses in a row, all were squatted, half of them by lesbians. The woman at number 30 was 'straight', so I was told, and expecting me. I thought it would be a quick in and out, get the key and go; I'd travelled a long way hitch-hiking from

Lancaster, so wasn't really up for chit-chat with straight strangers.

Val, a big woman, answered the door to me and took me upstairs to her living room; everywhere was painted black, there were a few dim lights around the place. She spoke with a very posh voice, everything felt unfamiliar. When we got in the room there was a tall young black man sitting in the corner, he looked a bit embarrassed when he saw me, almost like I'd caught him not only rolling a joint but probably also trying to get his leg over with a big fat white woman. As if I'd be bothered. We both had to suffer Val going on and on about how good the weed was that she'd given him to roll. I was horrified at the disgusting tea she'd tried to poison me with as it tasted like the pink swill the dentist gives you to spit out. Oh well. I just wanted to leave and get away from her house and her manky tea. Two joints and no more cups of tea later I made my escape and arrived at my new abode, tired, thirsty and only slightly stoned.

Number 42 was a bit less squalid than number 30, for one thing it wasn't painted all black and it had a hall carpet. This was the first time I'd seen the house. My friend Gemma, who I knew from the scene in Lancaster, had moved in here not long before and Hannah my sister, like me a dyke, was moving in the following day. Val had told me that all the 'women' (the lesbians) were away at a women's conference for the weekend, somewhere out of town. I was a bit disappointed really as I'd quite fancied meeting lots of new women.

The house was quite cozy for a squat; it had beds, blankets, pillows and sheets, an outside toilet, a kitchen in the basement with a cooker and a table and chairs, but no bathroom. There was a small printed sign on the ceiling leading down to the basement which read, 'Ours is a nice house ours is': that made me smile when I read it. I took the ground floor as my bedroom; it was two rooms knocked through but only had an old feeble gas fire to keep the chill off. After I'd unpacked what little I needed for the night, I rolled a joint with my dope - not some hippy weed from down the road at number 30 - and got into bed with half my clothes on to stay warm and to keep the damp out.

The next day I slept in. When I got up I had another nosey around the house in the daylight, unpacked a bit more and then set off to meet Hannah at Victoria Coach station. She was only 18 years old and not as used to hitch-hiking as I was at the grand age of 22, so she'd got the coach down from Manchester. This was her leaving home for the first time. Mam had given me a check for £60 to help the two of us settle in and we paid her back a few months later.

Hannah was as keen as I was to meet other lesbians, so that night we decided to go to the Sol's Arms somewhere between Euston and Tottenham

Court Road. There was a women's disco every Saturday and Tuesday nights though I'd heard that Saturday wasn't the best night to go because the women who went there were what I called 'straight' dykes. They were more conventional and acted like heterosexual couples but in a way they were worse. They were either butch or femme and no-one was allowed to make eye contact for fear of stealing someone else's girlfriend and possibly getting your head kicked in. It wasn't really the kind of place you would go to chat and meet people. We only went because there was nowhere else to go and we were desperate to get out on the pull on our first night out in the big city.

Pumpkin time was fast approaching; the final record deadline. The furthest I'd got all night to anywhere near a bit of nooky was when a quite sloshed, pretty, femme woman had asked me to dance. I jumped at the chance only to have her girlfriend turn up sharpish to ward me off. So now me and Hannah were both pretty desperate for a shag. We scoured the edges round the dance floor for single women while all the married couples clung onto each other smooching to the Commodores' 'Three Times a Lady'. I didn't quite have the front to go up and ask complete strangers if they wanted to come back with us so I talked Hannah into doing it!

We picked out two fairly suitable women, mine was a white South African, as I found out in between our bouts of shagging. I was really surprised that she was a nice person as I suppose I would've been a bit more cautious about her if I'd known before we got in bed, what with all the trouble in South Africa. I had to give her one pound for her bus fare the next day as she didn't have enough to get all the way home. Hannah didn't have much luck with her one-night stand who didn't want to get undressed and would hardly speak to her.

Gemma came back on Sunday evening. She made a gorgeous meal which we ate, and then listened to her extensive music collection while relaxing in her bedroom. She laughed at our weekend escapades and we laughed at hers at the women's conference. Several joints and a few bottles of beer later, it was time to go to bed. I had to start a new job in the morning as an agency nurse at the Westminster Hospital right next to the Houses of Parliament. I'd qualified as a nurse over a year ago and swore I'd never go back to it, yet here I bleeding was again, hanging out my bastard uniform with its cut-throat stiff white collar and clammy black tights. Urgh! It made my flesh crawl.

So on Monday morning I got the bus to Aldgate and then waited for another bus to take me to Westminster. It took forever just to get a little bit of the way on this busy bus route and I was running seriously late. I couldn't be late on my first day, so I had to jump off the bus and use all the money I had on me to get a taxi, leaving me with no money for lunch or for the bus fare home. I just about made it to the nursing office on time. I had to report for duty to a nursing officer along with another agency nurse. Being a nurse was like being in the Army, what with officers, duty, different ranks, uniform and of course being spoken to like shit - let's not forget that.

Miss Springham sprung onto the other agency nurse.

'And where did you train, dear?' Miss Springham said in a voice that sounded like she was the Queen's cousin or summat.

'Oh, I trained at Guy's,' the agency nurse said, like she was the Queen's niece.

'Oh really, and do you know blah de blah?' Miss Springham said, thrilled with her assumed royal relation.

'Oh yahsie, yahsie,' the agency nurse replied equally thrilled at the royal connection.

I stood there smiling naively, waiting for my turn to speak. When the royal nurses had finally spat out a pound of plums at each other, Miss Springham turned to me.

'And where did you train, dear?' she said.

'Lancaster,' I replied in my normal northern accent.

As quick as she had turned to ask me her question, she turned her head away and said, 'Never mind dear'.

And that was that. She hated me from then onwards. I soon came to realize that the Westminster Hospital was probably the most prestigious hospital in the country (excluding the private ones of course). It sat quietly next to the Houses of Parliament, right opposite the Archbishop of Canterbury's official residence Lambeth Palace. There were lots of huge Ministry of Defence buildings nearby and a large number of MoD patients attended the orthodontics department where I worked (we did things that ordinary dentists can't do). I did other clinics as well occasionally.

There was a nice non-royal nurse in orthodontics, I was taking over from her. She noticed I had nothing to eat at dinner time so gave me some of her food and after I told her about having to get a taxi she gave me 50p to get me home. I didn't have enough money at home to pay her back and have the fare to get home again the next day and I couldn't get to a bank. Hannah didn't have any money either, so I was fretting like mad.

The next morning when I was about to leave for work, a letter popped through the letterbox. It was addressed to me so I shoved it in my pocket and headed off to work. I carried on fretting like mad all the way: I couldn't not give the nurse her 50p but the thought of walking all that way home was so daunting. I didn't even know the way and it hung over me like a dark cloud the whole journey into work. When I got off the bus I thought, 'Oh well I might as well open this letter.' Normally I'd be thrilled to get any post and open it immediately. It was a hand-written letter with a London postmark but who could it be from? I was slightly interested now at this bit of distraction. I opened the letter and a pound note fell out. I couldn't believe it. Who the hell would send me a pound note, especially on the very day that I so desperately needed one? I couldn't believe my eyes. Could it be from god himself?

'Dear Cec,

Here's a pound for all the ear-bashing and moralistic claptrap that you've had to suffer all your life in my name, sorry it's only a £1 when it should be a trillion trillion.

Not yours anymore,

God.'

But no, it wasn't from god after all. It was from the South African woman I'd shagged on Saturday. I couldn't believe it. I didn't even know she knew the name of our street, never mind the number. She thanked me for a nice night and for giving her the money to get home with. I was happy again, yippee!

Kate, my ex-girlfriend, was moving down to London from Lancaster on Friday. We were supposed to move down together but she finished with me two weeks ago, on St Valentine's Day. Hannah made a snap decision and moved down with me instead. Kate had come to do a degree in nursing at St. Thomas'; she already had a degree but wanted to be a nurse for some insane reason. She was moving into the nurses' home at the weekend.

St. Thomas' was on one side of Lambeth Bridge and the Westminster Hospital was on the other side. You move all the way to London and get a job next door to your ex, by coincidence as well. I was anxious about her moving down to London, but also desperate to see her. I was very much in love with Kate. We'd been together for two years and most of the time we'd lived with each other. She was exactly one year younger than me and very, very beautiful. I didn't really know why we'd split up; there was always something or other going on with her. Recently the inside of my head was battered to pieces from the emotional roller coaster ride that being Kate's girlfriend involved. I slept with someone else a few days after Kate had chucked me and now I'd slept with that South African woman. I suppose they both acted as very slight antidotes towards curing the dreadful pain I felt from my split with Kate. I was counting the days and nights until her arrival in this massive city, a city that felt tiny while it too waited for her to descend upon it.

Another mad coincidence had happened. As I looked out of my bedroom window, there at the end of the garden was the back of a pub. It was called the British Prince and was frequented by a load of ex-student socialists and communists. A number of them were straight friends of Kate's who she knew from Lancaster University. I was pissed off by the intrusion. I thought at long last I could live in a straight-free zone and here they bleeding were, right outside my bedroom window. Kate and I had had a lot of opposition from so-called 'right-on' left wing people; they were never brave enough to say it to your face but it was always there nevertheless. At the same time as being fed up with them being there, I was also pleased because apart from me, Hannah and Gemma, they were Kate's only other contacts in London and I knew she would probably come over to the pub to see them, possibly this weekend. Just the thought of her being so close by sent huge shockwaves through my body that ended up stabbing at my heart. I felt like I had to swerve my mind away from even thinking about her. Although it was only two weeks since I'd last seen her it felt like a lifetime. I'd never gone this long without seeing her since we had first met.

Hannah and I went to the Sol's Arms on Tuesday night for the 'better' women's disco with some of the women from our street. We met loads of new women, all friendly and keen to meet us and we had a really good night out. Some of the women from our street went to the British Prince. They said it was good, and there was an Asian man who played the piano and sang 'leftie' songs which is why so many young socialists and communists went there. They said Thursday was a good night so I thought, as Kate wasn't coming down till Friday, it would be safe to go that Thursday. So off we went to the dreaded British Prince, or the B.P. as Hannah came to call it.

As soon as we went through the door I liked it. The atmosphere was lively, all the socialists looked lit up by someone singing their songs out loud and playing their music. There were more lesbians than I thought there would be. A group of them lived a few streets away in other squats and they were here mingling with the local straight lefties, who appeared more respectful on the surface to lesbians than the Lancaster lot I'd met. Maybe they'd had more practice, or maybe it was because I'd stolen Kate from the Lancaster lot - she was straight before we got together.

I spotted a couple of Kate's friends in the distance. I kept my eye contact minimal but by the end of the night they were all over me.

'Oh, hiya Cec, Kate said you lived around here,' one of them said. She was intrigued, by the lesbian circus that had accompanied me. All her friends knew how besotted I was with her. 'It's a great pub, isn't it? Are you coming down tomorrow?' Kate's friend continued.

'Hmm, I don't know.' I said.

'It should be a good night,' the friend said.

I don't know how I came to be in the B.P. on the Friday night that Kate finally landed in London. It was one of those heart-teetering moments that spread out the whole night. I had a ton of support from Hannah and Gemma, and the other women in our street seemed to really like me and Hannah so they came out with me as well. The pub was very busy as usual. My spies spotted Kate, deep in the crowd of communists and socialists at the other end of the bar. My heart pounded and my nerves shook just knowing that she was in the same city, never mind the same room.

There were quite a few of us standing chatting outside our front door after the pub shut as we were near enough to the pub to have people walk past our door as they left to go home. Kate was in a big group of people who stopped near our house to chat. I was so nervous. I'd had no eye contact with her all night and suddenly here she was standing outside my front door, albeit surrounded by loads of people. Before her crowd had left she somehow managed to get past everyone and stand next to me. She had love in her eyes for me again. I was very surprised as the last time we saw each other it was completely over between us and yet here she was, loving me. I was thrilled but my heart let out a deep groan. 'Not more heartache Cecily', it said. Kate went off into the night with her happy group of friends.

Kate came over to see me and be part of the Stepney lesbian scene the following week. The nurses' home at St. Thomas' gave each resident just one small room, looking right down on the Houses of Parliament on the opposite bank of the river. I knew how lonely nurses' homes can be, having lived in one a few years previously, and I was desperate to spend every second with Kate. I loved her more than any words could say. Although we slept together that one time, I knew really that we weren't back together so my heavy heart had to creak on at her mercy.

After Kate left on Sunday morning, Hannah and I went to another local pub, the Silver Jubilee or the 'Jube' as we came to call it, with some of the women in our street. We'd been in a couple of times during the week for a game of pool and seen the landlord at a distance but today was a different matter. It wasn't wildly busy this particular day; we must have been the biggest group of people in together, about eight of us in all. We played pool constantly on the five pool tables that were spread out on one side of the big pub. Bill the landlord was a working-class East Ender in his early 60s who used to be a boxer. He knew all the other women who were with us and he smiled in such a friendly way at me and Hannah, making us feel at ease in this very rough area of the East End that lay on the edge of the docks. When the other customers had all gone, and we were about to leave, he gave us all a free pint each, then another and another. We all just chatted, drank and played pool all afternoon and well into the evening. I kept thinking he was going to turn all weird and pervy at any moment, but no, he was just lovely and gentle all the time we were there and ever after as well. He used to say, 'Anyone gives you any trouble, you just tell me'. At weekends, they had a disco further down the room from all the pool tables and you had to pay if you wanted to stay and play pool late while the disco was on. Bill said, 'When they come round and ask you if you're staying, just say no so you don't have to pay and then stay'.

It was very rough. There was a seamen's mission just up the road and some of those sea-crazed men used to come to the pub. It's funny 'cos we never really had any trouble from the regular faces that we'd see, it was always the outsiders. The lesbians wouldn't go into the disco part, it was sacred ground really. I suppose it was where all the locals copped off with each other at the weekends so it was a dangerous place for us. We were only just tolerated playing pool and that was with the landlord offering us full protection.

Two weeks later, Gemma had invited some of our friends from Lancaster down to stay for the weekend. They turned up at the pub, the Jube on Saturday daytime, with an entourage of women from Hackney. Hannah and I joined them for what we thought was a lunchtime drink. This time Bill didn't serve all day so we took everyone back to ours. Gemma had a fantastic bedroom for any place, let alone a squat. Some previous squatter had built a raised wooden platform for a bed, plus a desk and shelves, all tailor-made for the room. She'd made it really nice as well. She had a great selection of music and like all of us liked to party. One of the women from Hackney had brought some cannabis oil with her, quite a rarity really and very strong. We all clubbed together and got a couple of bottles of tequila and drank, smoked and screamed laughing for the rest of the afternoon. Hannah wasn't used to tequila parties. She didn't know the Lancaster women as well as I did as she hadn't lived there like me so she bowed out soon after the party started. Sarah, one of the women from the Lancaster entourage, had recently become single. I'd always got on well with her, she was tall and very attractive, and had recently moved back down from Lancaster to London where she was originally from.

As soon as the pub opened at 5 o'clock, the party moved from Gemma's room to the Jube forthwith. The oil didn't smell like other dope so all we had to do was spread it down the outside of a cigarette, so we could carry on smoking joints even in the pub. Back onto lager again in the pub, by 6 o'clock I was getting shit-faced, as was everyone else. Hannah turned up stone cold sober just after six. She said that Sally, a woman I'd slept with just before I left Lancaster, had phoned up to say she was not only in London, but also on her way over to the pub. I'd only has sex with her once about a month ago, not long before I'd moved down here, but even then she'd sent me a bunch of flowers the next day via Interflora. I'd had no contact with her for weeks and here she was coming over uninvited. And worst still I was shit-faced and deep in intimate conversation with Sarah, who had been getting more and more attractive as the day went by. Oops, I was too drunk and stoned at this point to put anything into perspective, or even to give a shit about Sally harassing me by turning up unannounced.

6:30pm prompt Sally arrived, she was trying to act casual but was her usual bonkers self. I greeted her in a friendly enough way after I'd managed to prize myself loose from the heavenly hold of Sarah's laughter and gaze. Sally knew Sarah a bit from Lancaster, so she sat down in what I drunkenly thought was a comfortable way. We laughed, me and Sarah did anyway, and talked for a while and in what seemed like no time at all, Sally tipped the table over on us and stormed out of the pub. I didn't give a shit about her doing that. I wasn't the slightest bit annoyed as I'd had more than a bellyful of trouble and heartache from Kate, without anyone else adding to it. I was in my element being in Sarah's company all day. I didn't really care about anything else and of course the alcohol and drugs helped me to not give a shit. After our table was overturned, and in our drunken stupidity, we all decided to move out of the pool playing side of the pub and into the dangerous disco side. There were only two men in at this point, as it was still very early.

Not long after we sat down Sarah asked me if I wanted to dance. The dance floor was deserted, so the two of us got up and danced with our arms around each other. If we hadn't been so out of it, we would have burst into flames with the evil eyes of the two men at the bar burning into us. After we'd finished our dance we went to the bar for yet another drink - we were stood right next to the two men. Sarah hadn't noticed them at all and although I was very drunk I never lost my danger radar. I suppose at the back of my mind I knew that the rest of our big entourage would jump in and fight if needs be. We both smiled at the two men and one of them said to Sarah, 'Are you the man?' - she looked nothing like a man. She thought he'd said, 'Are you alright?' so she smiled and said 'Yeah'. He looked very puzzled by her answer. I thought she'd said it just for a laugh and hadn't realized that she'd simply misheard him. We sat down and screamed laughing when I told her what he'd really said.

We all went back to the pool-playing side of the pub, as a few more had started to come into the disco, and a fight would have broken out for sure if we'd stayed. The next thing I remember is waking up, with me sat up in my bed, very surprised to find Sarah asleep under one arm, a bucket under the other and a half smoked joint in my hand. I had no recollection of getting into bed with Sarah but I knew we mustn't have had sex as I definitely would've remembered that. I was very embarrassed. Apart from Sally and the South African woman, I'd only slept with Kate for the past two years, and not that many women before then really. Sarah woke up and laughed when she saw me with my arm around the bucket and the half-smoked joint in me hand. She said that the bucket was for her 'cos she'd felt sick, probably from smoking the joint on top of everything else we'd had. Thank god it hadn't caught fire while we were asleep.

I got up to make us a cup of tea and found out from Hannah that Sally had had to sleep in her bed with her, 'cos she had nowhere else to stay. Sally had then got up early to catch the train back home.

Some of the Lancaster entourage stayed in Gemma's room and were still partying and god knows what else. I brought the tea back to bed and wanted to get up because I was too shy to be in bed with such a gorgeous woman. But Sarah chatted and laughed so freely with me that it wasn't long before we slipped under the sheets together.

The Ghost Train

We had lovely neighbors next door at number 40 (joke). They were a mother and daughter and they both worked as prostitutes. The mother, Enid, was small, plump, with bleached blonde hair. She was rough and mad as hell. Her daughter Gill was mixed race and stunningly attractive. She turned up to a lesbian party on our street once wearing just one leather glove and a trilby. She held the gloved hand up all night as she paraded around the room like it was some kind of fanny magnet. It worked as well, she took a poor unsuspecting woman back home and while she was in bed 'humping this bird' (Gill's words not mine) Gill's boyfriend walked in on them. The bird flew out as quickly as she could. I think the boyfriend wanted a threesome - yuck.

There were men knocking on their door day and night. I don't think they were capable of running a proper brothel as such - they were too crazy. They would shout and argue with the men, with each other and with us. Enid would call her daughter Gill a black cunt and she'd call us white, dirty, lezzie honkies even though she was white. She threw notes over the garden fence calling us amongst other things, 'fanny fingering fuckers' which we thought was the funniest thing ever. We looked forward to the notes 'cos we would literally cry laughing. That was until she started to smear them with dog shit. One of the notes was on House of Commons' note paper, which surprised me 'cos I couldn't see them making any high connections. It must have been the daughter Gill as she was a tiny bit calmer than her mother.

I was at the bus stop one day with my nurse's gabardine on over my uniform. I was going to work on a late shift and there were quite a few people waiting for the bus as well. The next thing I knew Enid and her daughter were walking towards the bus stop. As soon as they spotted me Enid started shouting at me.

'I bet they don't know that you're fucking queer at the hospital, do they?'

She and her daughter roared laughing. Everyone at the bus stop looked at me, and then quickly looked away. I kept my head held high and looked at as many people in the eye as possible. I thought any one of you could end up being a patient of mine at some point in the future - your life or one of your relatives could be in my hands, so watch it. Everyone seemed embarrassed and Enid and Gill just ended up showing themselves up. I'd like to say they felt worse than me, but I was mortified and they were too crazy to feel any normal emotions.

Another time they'd left their front door open for two days and nights. Some of us from our street were curious as to what was going on - had they been burgled or, worse still, murdered? It had been a bit of a boring weekend at the time as Gemma had broken her leg in a motorbike accident a couple of weeks before, so we had to hang around at home to keep her company. Anyway, by Sunday night curiosity and a lack of excitement took over and about five of us decided to venture inside Enid's house and investigate what, if anything, had happened. You've never seen anything like the state of their house - really tacky leopard skin throws everywhere you looked. It wasn't scummy dirty, just hideous really. We clung together and poked our heads around the upstairs bedroom doors, not knowing what we'd find. We were hyped up and a bit hysterical as we looked around from room to room. All of a sudden we heard this terrible shouting from outside in the street - it was Enid.

'I've been fucking robbed. Them fucking lezzies are robbing me.' I've never moved so fast in my life. I shot towards the stairs only to find Gemma with her crutches trying to get down the stairs as quick as she could, which was too slow for me. In my panic to get out I pushed past her as the chances were Enid probably had some big fuck-off man or men with her. I had to save my own neck and get out before they came in and got me.

'Call the fucking police', Enid was still shouting on the street.

There was a black man with her, but he wasn't that big and was stood next to his car throwing up in the road. Phew, what a relief. We tried to explain to Enid that we were worried that something might have happened to her, 'cos her front door was wide open. We must've got through to her somehow 'cos she never phoned the police, thank god. There was never a dull moment in that street I can tell you.

A couple of months later Enid's front door had been left open again. We'd closed it and hadn't heard hide nor hair of her for what seemed like ages. We assumed she'd finally moved out - at long frigging last. An Asian family moved in and we thought that was that. They did the garden up and planted vegetables. We let them have half of our garden, they were a nice family. Peace at last from Enid's lunacy, or so we thought.

After a few weeks there was a knock at our front door. It was the Asian chap from next door looking very distressed. To our horror, Enid was stood out on the street shouting and swearing.

'These fucking Pakis have broken into me 'ouse. Somebody call the police.'

She kept shouting it over and over again. The poor Asian bloke couldn't speak English, but he still knew something horrendous was going on, and that he and his family could be about to lose their home. I started to panic. Being a very racist area, I thought that if the police do come, then they'll be racist and take Enid's crazy word over this nice man's. I envisaged a crowd gathering to come and see what all the fuss was about - a frigging racist mob. But mostly I feared the police. I felt a bit sick, what with this poor fucking family minutes away from being evicted. The police station was only just down the road at Leman Street. They'll be here any second and that'll be it. Sure enough a police car pulled up outside the house, and to my absolute joy, the police sergeant who got out was a tall handsome Asian man. I never thought I'd ever say this, but I've never been so pleased to see a copper in all my life. Enid shut the fuck up with her racism, as soon as she saw him.

I explained to the policeman that the house was a squat, and that Enid had not lived in it for months. This family had now moved in and were part of the housing co-op that was in this area. They weren't really, but the copper wasn't to know. I'd told Hannah to go quickly and get some of the other women on a nearby street, who were part of a housing co-op, so that they could verify my story. It was fair that they should live here - you can't just fuck off and leave a squat empty for months on end. I spoke clearly and calmly and put their case forward, quite well I thought. And that was it. Ta ta, finally, to Enid. The copper drove off and we never saw the lovely Enid again.

There was often an element of fear in the air, not from crazy Enid so much but from our position stuck on the edge of a massive white working-class housing estate and a huge tower block just a few yards down the road. The National Front was rife in Bethnal Green and Hackney at the time, which was only next door to our borough, and most people knew we were not only squatters but also queer. An Asian family lived a few doors down from us, a man and a woman in their early 30s with two kids. Some of the women from the pub, who hung about with the straight lefties, told us that the Asian man had been stabbed a few years earlier in a racist attack just down the road and had nearly died. The attacker had just been released from jail so could we keep an eye out for them, make sure they were safe? I was angry at the racist bastards. Being quite tall and fearless at times, I made sure that Hannah and I hung about on the street more of the time and stopped and chatted at every opportunity with the Asian family, even though neither of us could speak the other one's language. We smiled and nodded a lot and chatted to their kids on the doorstep. The fear on the man's face when we first stopped to chat was terrifying to see but all the dykes and the straight lefties kept a vigilant eye on them. The Asian squats on our street had wire mesh over the windows which was not surprising after that incident.

Barely a month had gone by when a poor Bengali man, Altab Ali, was attacked by a gang of racists, on Adler Street off Brick Lane, about a mile down the road from us. Sadly, the 25-year-old couldn't escape his vicious attackers and died in a nearby Whitechapel park, after being stabbed in the neck. On the day of his murder the National Front were standing for election in 43 council seats. In a BBC report Altab's friend, Shams Vladdin, said,

'Many other racist incidents were being ignored. It was very difficult for Bengali's to go out on their own, because they'd often been abused as well as having their windows smashed in. Altab Ali's death was the final straw, his blood made us realize we couldn't ignore it, or who would be next? We knew there would be no place for us unless we fought back.'

So everyone joined together and ten days after Ali's death, about 7,000 people marched behind his coffin through central London, calling on the government to address racism in East London. They marched to Hyde Park, Trafalgar Square and to Downing Street. Shams recalls the chants of 'Black and White Unite and Fight', as the large crowd moved through the streets. Change was far from immediate. Just one month later another

Asian man, Ishaque Ali, was killed in a racially motivated attack in nearby Hackney. Although it wasn't as bad for us lesbians, you still took your life in your hands, never knowing quite when some fucker was going to attack you.

One such time was when Kate, my straight sister Bernie and I were walking back from the pub on a Sunday afternoon. They were linking arms with each other and I was walking alongside them with a bag of cans and a couple of bottles of beer. The rest of our gang were out of sight. Two young men had followed us from the pub, and as they got nearer they started with the verbal homophobic abuse. The hackles on the back of my neck knew they were about to jump us from behind - everything seemed to go into slow motion. The second that one of them started to jump me, that was the second that I ducked down and put my hand in the bag, to search for one of the bottles amongst the cans. Bingo, I found it immediately and swung around on him pushing the bottle up to his face - boy was I angry. He shat himself! His accomplice dived back from us as well. I held the bottle at his face for a few seconds and roared at him.

'Come on, I thought you wanted a fucking fight', I said.

'No, no, we don't want any trouble', the big shit said holding both his cowardly arms up after he'd tried to attack a group of women from behind.

That was the second time Bernie had been on the receiving end of a homophobic attack and she wasn't even a dyke. The other time was a few years earlier in Lancaster, when a gang of Hell's Angels decided to come and sort the queers out once and for all at a local disco. Most of the people weren't gay at the disco, but the mere fact they were alive was enough to warrant an attack. Anyway, Bernie saw me getting my head kicked in and jumped into the fight to rescue me. I bet there's not many straight people who can say they've had two homophobic attacks against them - my beautiful loyal sister.

Although the streets of the East End could be rough, there were some things that I loved. Stepney was a very big Jewish area in its day and probably still was to a degree. I knew very little about Jews apart from what I'd heard at school and church. I was quite intrigued by the Jewish culture. Maybe it was the religious connection as being brought up by Irish Catholic parents opened me up to other cultures a bit more than my English peers. I wanted to see another way of life, to get to know something of these people with such a rich history - people who had survived the poverty of East End London and all its rich, gutsy working-class history. A lot of what were once big Jewish areas, like Whitechapel and Brick Lane, had changed in fairly recent years to a different group of immigrants - Asians. Most of the businesses had changed and the shops and markets sold different things in addition to what they used to sell. You could still get bagels twenty-four hours a day on Brick Lane amongst all the many Indian restaurants. There was Tubby Isaac's takeaway kiosk at the bottom of Whitechapel Road that sold Jewish food. You had to queue right down the street on a Sunday morning for bagels. In the bakery round the corner from us, there were probably more non-Jews queuing than Jews. Everybody loved bagels.

We had a Jewish woman come to visit us one day, well she'd come to visit the women at number 34 but they weren't in, so she knocked on our door. We'd already heard all about her from the other women, so we were pleased when she called at our house. Her name was Rebecca and she must've been in her late 50s or early 60s. She had dark shoulder-length hair sprinkled with grey, and long dark clothes. Apparently, she'd been in prison for bank robbery and was now on the run. I didn't know the ins and outs and didn't really want to. People had told me that she was always trying to recruit young women into the next heist. I suppose I was already a bit giddy by the time she got in the front room after I'd opened the door to her. In the back of my mind I was probably waiting for her to try and recruit me and Hannah and see what tactics she'd use to turn us into the Kray sisters of the East End.

Rebecca sat down for hours telling us this story and that story. I could've listened to her forever as she told us of the old East End; the Cable Street Riots only a few streets away from where we were, the Fascists against the Jews, the Trade Unions, this and that - it was ace. She asked us if we minded if she rolled a joint of grass. No, no, we said, we liked a smoke, so she skinned up and we smoked with her. Well, me and Hannah weren't used to smoking grass and the next thing we knew this little kitten, that Hannah had acquired, started to jump on top of Rebecca's chest to grab her dangling earing that had caught the light from outside. She went mad at the kitten and at us, because we were falling on the floor laughing and couldn't stop. The madder she got the more we laughed. When we managed to compose ourselves again and apologize for the kitten's behavior, we sat and listened to more stories. She couldn't see the kitten where she was but we could see it and the more she moved her head the more the earring caught the light. The kitten kept nodding its head up and down with each movement that Rebecca made with her head and we had to keep an eye on it in case it jumped on her again. Her stories suddenly seemed more serious than they probably were, and the harder we tried to control our absolute hysteria the worse it was. Of course, the kitten jumped on her again, by which time me and Hannah had totally collapsed over the couch, just sobbing with laughter till it hurt. Rebecca wasn't happy with us for laughing so much. The odd time I'd bump into her she was always very pleased to see me, and often told people how hospitable Hannah and I were the day she came to visit. We only really saw her at parties as she had to be careful where she went socially, because so many police and screws (as she put it) would be a part of the lesbian scene.

We were always screaming laughing in our house - it was like we were in a constant cabaret. Mari, who I'd known only slightly from Lancaster, was now living down here. She was always at our house; she was around almost every day. She was a month to the day younger than me and both me and Hannah got on very well with her. We always had such great craic with her even though she was quite shy and unassuming. One day she had come round to see us after work. The three of us were sat around the kitchen table with a cup of tea - we hadn't been laughing or talking about anything in particular. All we did was put the cups of tea up to our mouths and we all got hysterical, laughing for no reason other than that. We had to spit the tea out, we were so hysterical. Another time, Mari told us of the day she was upstairs on a bus with a plastic curtain rail she'd bought. She had to hold it up vertically 'cos there was nowhere else to put it and each time a person got up from their seat, or walked past the rail, they automatically grabbed hold of it. Of course, it just kept bending and they kept falling around, much to the great amusement of everyone on the bus. She said that just when things would settle down from one person doing it then it would happen again, for the whole length of her journey. It could only happen to her.

We didn't have a bath at our house, just a little electric water heater over the kitchen sink. We had to have a strip wash quite often in front of visitors. I wasn't that bothered really, I was more bothered about going round dirty than people seeing me wash me fanny! Down the road at number 46 they had a bath, the only one of the lesbian houses which did, so there'd always be a queue on a Friday night. A woman called Eve lived there who was a bit of an oddball, I suppose she was lonely more than anything else. Sometimes she would turn up at our house, sit in the kitchen and just say nothing. She turned up once with a massive floppy pink hat and a half-drunk small bottle of whisky. She looked absolutely bonkers and was desperately trying to make some kind of conversation with us. Of course, we thought it was really funny, her turning up like this and we could barely keep a straight face. I tried to avoid having a bath there because she would always be hanging around and making up excuses for why she had to come in the bathroom while you were in there. Weirdo. After a while an American woman called Lucy moved into number 46. We got on well, so I didn't mind going round there for a bath so much anymore as Eve behaved herself when Lucy moved in.

There was a constant trickle of women moving in and out of the five houses squatted by dykes on our street. Two such women were Amy and Teresa, nick-named by Hannah as Midge and Madge, who moved into number 26. Teresa was Irish, nice but a bit too intense sometimes. Amy looked like an army doctor from the 1950s with her old-fashioned glasses and hairstyle. She was pleasant enough, just a bit of a drip really and slightly jolly hockey sticks. The mainstays of the street's women were Vicky and Alex, who lived at number 34. Alex had been there a couple of years while Vicky used to live at our house and had then moved in with Alex, her 'lover' (people didn't seem to say girlfriend down here). You couldn't even say you fancied someone without getting a feminist ear-bashing despite 'fancy' meaning sexual attraction between two people. I quite rightly ear-bashed anyone back who tried to tell me their weird beliefs on how I should live.

Vicky and Alex seemed to be the unofficial leaders of the 'lesbian liberation movement'. They'd had a women's band and Alex had a book printed in the early seventies. She and another woman interviewed lesbians and put what they had to say in a book. It was quite liberating at the time - I don't think anyone had done anything like it before. Alex and some other women had a photograph made into a poster of about five women posing with toy rifles and in no time at all their house was raided by some heavy police department, thinking that they were some kind of lesbian terrorists. This all happened before we moved down.

The police were hot on finding terrorists. Not only was the IRA rife in the '70s but there were anarchist terrorist groups throughout Europe, and some of these groups were known to have lesbians in them. Probably the most famous group seemed to be led by a woman, the Baader-Meinhof Gang. They were German and had killed a lot of people. Most were captured but there were still some of the group on the run. One night only a few months after I'd moved down, I went out to the pub on my own. I'd been working a late shift as a nurse and it was about 9:30pm and still light and humid. Everyone else was already in the pub. I had a white T-shirt, black cotton trousers and my adorable slick, black, leather motorbike jacket on. It was a Friday and I couldn't wait to start the weekend, when all of a sudden a car pulled up next to me on the main road. There were four men in dark clothes inside the car - it all happened very quickly. One of them jumped out of the car and grabbed me from behind. He had his arm around my neck and was trying to drag me into the car. I started shouting and struggling to get away and then I realized they were police.

'What you doing this for? I'm a nurse. I've just finished a late shift. I'm only going out to the pub.'

In my quick thinking I appealed to the empathy that the police and hospital staff had for each other. Without saying anything, he let me go, got back in the car and drove off with the others who had all stayed in the car. This was the second time this had happened to me. The other time was when I was hitch-hiking at a motorway slip road a few years before. A car pulled up in the same way. A policeman, with a uniform on under his coat, grabbed me and tried to drag me into a car just like this time. On that occasion it turned out to be a case of mistaken identity - they were looking for a man with white trousers and a black coat. As soon as I opened my mouth they just laughed and explained the mix up but this time I didn't even get a reaction, never mind anything else. I was really mad at the harassment I'd received.

The next day in the papers it was all over the headlines and on the telly - they had arrested a German woman called Astrid Proll who was a former member of the Baader-Meinhof Gang. She was a lesbian and they'd picked her up in Hackney about two miles from us. Not only that but they were on the look-out for another lesbian terrorist in the area. The connection between Astrid Proll's arrest and me being caught in a stranglehold didn't click till I told my Mam about it a few weeks later. Apparently, Astrid Proll was known on the Hackney scene where she'd changed her name to Anna and had become a car mechanic. Mari knew her a bit. She said she was just a nice gentle German woman in Hackney at the time. Nobody had any idea that Anna the Spanner, as she was affectionately known, was really Astrid Proll, international terrorist gang member. I used to hear of this person and that person belonging to this and that organization from time to time, but I always told whoever the teller was to stop talking, because I didn't want to know anything about it. I knew how easy it was for people to be wrongly accused of things, and what dangerous times it could be politically.

Kate hadn't been in touch with me for what seemed ages before I slept with Sarah though it was probably only a couple of weeks. The one time I managed to speak to her on the phone I more-or-less met a brick wall. Silly me for thinking I was of the slightest interest to her. Never mind the two years we had together as wife and wife. It was only after she found out that I had slept with Sarah that she'd got in touch with me. Sarah was quite a catch in a lot of women's eyes; she was tall, gorgeous-looking, good fun and an all-round very nice woman. Kate would've found out from the Lancaster/London grapevine as there were a lot of ex-Lancaster University students in London, gay and straight.

Kate came over on a Wednesday with a great darkness over her, despite her delicate smiles. We arranged to go and see Patti Smith in concert, at the Rainbow in Finsbury Park, on Saturday night. She never mentioned Sarah but I could tell she knew something; I was used to her keeping everything locked up in the sadness of her mind. The phone went while she was there - it was Sarah and she wanted to see me on Saturday. I too had become sad and a bit dark after barely any time with Kate. If it would hurt her for me to go out with Sarah at any time, then it would hurt me too. That's how it was for me. I told Sarah that me and Kate were going out on Saturday and she was very nice about it as she liked Kate. Kate and I slept together on the Wednesday and Saturday night; we just held each other.

Kate came over to the Jube on the following Friday. She was on good form, playing pool with me, having a laugh, loving, anyone would've thought we were back together, even me for that matter. I was walking on sunshine. But by the time Sunday evening came around and she had to say goodbye, she'd turned flighty and said maybe we shouldn't really get back together. I couldn't believe it; the amount of times we'd been back to square one was unreal. My heart was ground to powder.

'Just go', I said, too shaken to barely stand, never mind speak.

Next I heard of her was over a week later. While I was in the Jube she'd been in the B.P. where she'd been playing pool with a fuck-ugly Australian woman who was staying with Vicky and Alex at no 34. We only went in the B.P. the odd time, mostly everyone went to the Jube. She was obviously avoiding me. I didn't find out till the next morning and I was absolutely blazing - not only was she in bed with another woman but she was only a few yards down the road from me. It was like a giant multiple-sided sword had been stabbed through my entire body and had landed right outside number 34's front door.

I was so distraught; I just wanted to kill them. Hannah and Gemma tried to dissuade me from going down to the house but I could barely see them, never mind hear what they were saying. I knocked at number 34. Another Australian woman answered, who was staying with her girlfriend, but they weren't with the ugly fuck. I liked this woman Louise, who opened the door, she already knew something was up. She invited me into the basement kitchen and offered me some breakfast. She was very calm and pleasant. Her girlfriend came in; she was really nice as well. I couldn't feel too murderous with them being so lovely. I think they were pissed off with the whole thing themselves and totally understood my distress.

They obviously loved each other very much, so could empathize with me, 'My loved one shagging someone else right under my nose' is not something most people want to experience.

The rest of the house was extremely quiet while the three of us cooked breakfast. We never mentioned anything about why I was there or what had happened - they just knew. It was almost like I had been hit with a tranquilizer dart the second Louise opened the door to me. I imagine that the guilty parties had either frozen to ice in fear, or crept out of the house with their lives in their hands knowing that I might really kill them. Either way, I never heard a creak and I was listening alright, I can tell you. I tried to carry on my life as best I could but it was a horrible blow to have all that happen to me. Most of the last few months with Kate had been an emotional roller-coaster but now it was turning into the ghost train, crashing into the house of horrors. I didn't know if I could cope with much more. Hannah and Gemma pulled together to become one big rock for me - I would never have survived it all without them two.

Just when I thought it couldn't get any worse, a couple of Fridays later Kate and the fuck-ugly Australian turned up in the Jube together. Kate had a fake fur coat on that I hadn't seen before. She looked like a classy film star, a modern-day Audrey Hepburn. The Australian quite a bit older than her and really was unattractive. All my lights automatically lit up, like a giant pinball machine pinging around my head whenever I saw Kate. This time my heart started to cry when my eyes saw who she was with. I kept my cool and stayed in the pub. All the other women there more or less knew what was going on as I was more well-known to them now. The Australian was just a travelling woman who would probably be back to her nice Australian lifestyle in a matter of months. I was here to stay, for now anyway. I could see concern for me in most women's eyes.

It was a while after they arrived in the pub that Kate came to talk to me. I was away from the bar near the pool tables. She told me that she was leaving London in the next couple of weeks. She and the Australian were going to live together in Rome. I turned away from her and saw Hannah and Gemma at the bar - they had been watching my every move to make sure I was okay. I tried to walk towards them. I felt like my legs were going to give way on me with each step. I was desperately trying to hold myself together and not cry in front of the whole pub. Hannah and Gemma willed me towards them with their eyes and whole beings. It was the longest walk of my life, even though it was probably only about ten steps. By the time I arrived the floodgates had already opened, they each put an arm around me as I cried into them.

It was quite busy in the pub, so it was easier to keep my dignity without everybody seeing me. The three of us sat at a table that was at the front of the bar that separated the pool room and the disco. No one could see what we were up to. Mari turned up and came and joined us and we eventually ended up hysterical laughing like usual. Kate and the Australian didn't stay for very long. They didn't go to Rome either, or stay together for much longer. This was a mercy as far as I was concerned, seeing as how I had to walk past number 34 every time I went out anywhere.

The Gateways

Hannah and I had got to know some women who lived a few streets away from us. They were squatting a house that used to be a café and it still had the signs painted up above the window, 'Lil's Café'. A couple of women called Penny and Kay lived there. Their home was almost opposite the Jube and on the odd occasion we'd go back to theirs after the pub as Hannah was having a bit of a fling with Penny.

One night a few of us went back to theirs from the pub, including a tall, dark, long-haired, attractive, straight woman, married in fact. I'd noticed her giving me the twice-over a few times in the pub but I thought no, as attractive as she was, I didn't like sleeping with straight and bi-sexual women. Well this woman was having none of it, or should I say she wanted all of it! She talked for a long time with me, very inquisitive she was. I didn't mind. I liked talking in depth about things. I suppose I was flattered that she wanted to know so much about me as well. It was always important to me that people liked and respected my mind as much as my body. She was staying over at Lil's Café - I could've walked home on my own as it was very late, or I too could stay over.

Hannah and Penny had long gone to bed; there was only me and her for hours and hours. She'd told me that she was very attracted to me and that she'd never felt a sexual attraction to a woman before, so she wanted to do something about this attraction. I was highly offended by this heterosexual woman's comments. Typical straight woman, I thought. She wasn't the first straight woman to make such a stupid remark, treating lesbians like we are some sort of sick whim. And what a surprise 'cos I thought you were all really plain and ugly, and now I actually fancy one. Whatever next.

Daylight was starting to creep in telling us it was time to go to bed - there wasn't much left to talk about anyway. I could feel the sexual excitement steaming off her. It really was time to either walk home or stay there on a single mattress across from her single mattress. I decided to stay. I didn't have to have sex with her. I didn't want to have sex with her after she'd made that comment earlier. Anyway, she had sex with men - how revolting's that. I didn't even fancy her. That big fat lie blobbed around the room and hid whenever it could. We walked into the bedroom next to the room we were already in, the room was full of fresh morning daylight; we undressed in its rays. Completely naked we got into our separate single beds. Most lesbians wouldn't get undressed and be completely naked for the first time right in front of each other, never mind this married woman. She had a beautiful body which probably made it easier for her to do it. We both just laid in our separate beds staring at the ceiling in silence. I couldn't bear the pressure of not shagging her, so I looked over at her, beckoned her into my bed with my eyes and pulled back the covers. Penny told me she went home the next day and told her husband that she was a lesbian. She also went into work on Monday morning and came out to everybody. I didn't sleep with her again.

After a couple of months as a nurse at the Westminster Hospital's orthodontics department I moved over the river to St Thomas' where Kate worked. It wasn't my decision; you had to take what the agency offered. It wasn't too bad because she was in nursing school for a few months while I was there, so I never saw her apart from one time when I popped into the nurses' home for a shag - we were back together briefly. I could see the Houses of Parliament out of the window while we were making love.

On one side of the main entrance hall of the hospital was a massive statue of Florence Nightingale, who had some big connections with the place, and right opposite her was a massive statue of Queen Victoria. It made me laugh, the irony of these two huge figures sitting looking at each other day and night. Florence Nightingale the lesbian and Queen Victoria who wouldn't pass a law making lesbianism illegal, because she couldn't believe it existed. I had visions of them coming to life from the stone and walking down off their high platforms in the middle of the night, when all the hustle and bustle of this busy hospital had died down. The two of them just chatting about life and their differences in a totally laidback, easy way, woman to woman.

St Thomas' was also a very prestigious hospital, not only did it have the Florence Nightingale connection but parts of it were very old. One ward that I worked in used to be the policemen's ward which probably dated from the turn of the century. You could still see some of the features from that time. People came from all over the world to be treated at this huge hospital, so big that the agency nurses went into a pool of nurses each day to see which ward needed a spare nurse. I had to report to the nursing office at the beginning of each shift to find out where I was needed. Again, because the hospital was so big they didn't just have one or two nursing officers (assistant matrons) but a whole big team of them. The very first time I had to report for duty, I arrived in my black leather jacket, t-shirt and trousers. Not only was it such a lezzie outfit, but also I had the double woman's symbol lesbian badge on my T-shirt for boldness. I walked along the corridor from the lift towards the nursing officer's office. I looked down to see about eight women nursing officers stood together. Every single one of them looked up at me in silence, not one batted an eyelid, not only at my blatant exposed lesbianism, but also the casualness of my attire. If it wasn't for their freaky-looking uniforms, then I could've sworn I was in a lesbian club. Anytime I had to have dealings with any one of them, I made sure that I gave them extra eye contact, slow and deliberately subtle teasing. I loved it. You could never have cracked them, well, years down the line maybe. Not that I ever would've wanted to - I just did it to relieve the boredom really, and I wanted them to come out.

Most of the nurses were 'yaisie yaisie', they'd say things like, 'Are you in a terry hurry?' meaning terrible hurry. It was like being in a 1940s film set. They were nice enough but cor blimey, a bit too surreal for me. One day I was going to lunch with a couple of nurses from my ward, and while we were in the lift one of them turned to me, and in her really posh voice said, 'Have you seen my nightingale?' I thought, don't tell me she's got a bird in the lift with her. I started to look around the ceiling of the lift. But no, the nurses at St Thomas' had different shaped hats to most other nurses and they called them their nightingales. I really chuckled to myself when I realized she'd meant her hat and not a poor nightingale bird trapped in the lift with us.

On nearly every ward that I worked in, which was probably every single one in the hospital, there would be someone or other high up in the

British Establishment. Lady this or Lord that, this MP, that army major; you name it this was the place to be if you had money and were ill. The top floor of the north wing was all private and the patients had their own rooms. There was a 12-year-old prince from Qatar in one room, with an armed guard on the door. His mother and aunt were with him and they frightened the life out of me when I first saw them because they had their faces covered with what looked like giant beaks. I'd never seen anything like it before and wasn't used to it.

Another time, also in a private room, I had to listen to a Tory MP's wife saying to a group of nurses that she had to go private because she couldn't bear to be in a ward with Auntie Mabel and Uncle Fred. She seemed to think that not only was it okay to say that to us, but also that it was funny and we should join in laughing. Most of the nurses were laughing. One of them was Asian and when she left the room this Tory wife started on the Asians. I thought right lady muck, how dare you slag off not only working-class people like me, but now you're starting on the Asians. Never mind that we're here looking after you so well on NHS wage rates at that, but you think it's okay to slag us off and still expect us to look after you with such dignity. She thought she would endear herself to us by chatting and making us laugh. When I got out of the room I told the Asian nurse what she had said about the Asians, because I knew that she was always lovely to the patients, and that she should reserve her loveliness when dealing with Mrs Tory MP. She looked really hurt and shocked when I told her what she'd said.

One day while I was on an afternoon shift, we all heard a terrible rumble from outside. Rumor went round that a bomb had gone off at Lambeth Palace which was right next to the hospital. I wasn't worried because I felt safe while I was still on duty, but when I finished my shift at 4.30pm it was a different story. I walked out of the hospital and onto Westminster Bridge as usual to catch the tube at the other side of the bridge. When I got to the station entrance, a few yards from Big Ben and the Houses of Parliament, there was a policeman standing guard, with loads of police tape sealed all over the tube station entrance. The atmosphere around me was one of silence and terrible fear. I shat myself. What the hell had happened? How was I going to get home now the tube was shut? I was starting to panic. I soon realized that a bomb had gone off much nearer than Lambeth Palace and I needed to get the fuck out of there. The solitary policeman's face didn't look good; he looked a bit shocked as well. I felt sick and couldn't work out how to get home or which direction to go in. I started to walk up river towards the Embankment in a blind panic, terrified that more bombs might go off. Eventually I arrived home having walked to the next tube station. I was very shaken.

The bomb had gone off in the MPs' car park at the Houses of Parliament; the pedestrian entrance was past and through the tube station, which I walked through every day to and from work. An MP, the Northern Ireland Secretary Airey Neave, had been blown to pieces in his car by the IRA just yards from where I was standing. Two months earlier there had been an explosion at the oil terminal at Canvey Island and we thought it was the end of the world. The night sky suddenly turning bright orange terrified us. My nerves were shattered by both these bombs.

Vicky and Alex from number 34 decided to take me and Hannah and a few others down to the famous Gateways Lesbian Club. Ever since we'd been down in London we couldn't wait to go there so here we were being escorted over to the opposite side of the city. The official line to gain entry to this so-called 'secret club' was that you had to be a member. Of course, me and Hannah weren't and neither were Vicky and Alex really, but because Alex had a book published she was famous enough to gain entrance. The plan was that they would ring the bell, go down the stairs followed by the rest of us and get waved through into the club. I'd decided to put a bit of someone's mascara on that night, something I never normally do. It felt so special to be finally going to the famous Gateways Club, the club that was in the first ever lesbian film, *The Killing of Sister George*, that I thought a bit of glamour was in order. I've never worn mascara since, I don't think. Anyway, the very butch woman at the bottom of the stairs waved our group through one by one, but when she got to me she put her arm in front of me to block my entrance.

'These can come,' she said looking at the rest of the group, 'but he can't', she said, looking at me.

A younger pretty woman who was also on the door, jumped in front of her as quick as a flash and pulled her arm down away from me.

'Smithy,' she said, 'get off her. Don't be so stupid. Of course she's a woman.'

Vicky and Alex and the rest of the gang all gathered around me. An older dark-haired feminine woman, who I later found out was Gina, the owner, sat up from her stool at the bar to clock everything because Alex was a bit of a celebrity. Gina didn't want someone in her party to be chucked out I suppose.

Smithy was still giving me the evils, like a male dog defending its territory - she definitely wasn't for letting me in. I undid my white cotton shirt completely, and pulled it wide open to reveal my breasts.

'There you are, I'm a woman. Satisfied?' I said defiantly.

'Have you had an operation?' Smithy said, looking like she was about to kill me.

'What?!', I shouted at her.

The pretty woman grabbed her and two other butch women came over to scuffle her off. I wouldn't have minded but she looked far more like a man than I did. We found out later that she was very pissed, even though it wasn't that late. I must have sparked a terrible jealous reaction inside of her. The other staff couldn't apologize enough.

We had a cracking night despite that incident; it was more of a laugh really. Hannah and I were half hoping that we would get to pull, but the women weren't really our type; they were a bit like the Saturday night Sol's Arms lot - straight, butch/femme types.

There were always places to go that were women-only nightclubs, like Junes and Spats or more alternative places which we preferred. The Woman's Art Alliance near Regent's Park, the Drill Hall off Tottenham Court Road - political women's social events were a regular occurrence. I hated the way everything had to be over by 11.30pm though, except in the clubs and the Jube of course. Sometimes people would come back to our house and we would have a laugh and a sing-song and get stoned. Hannah would play her guitar and we would usually start off singing Joan Armatrading songs like 'Somebody Who Loves You'. Mari would join in with the harmonies and it sounded really lovely when we could be serious for long enough. We'd often change the words of songs for a laugh, or make words up to the Blues; we certainly knew how to entertain our guests, that's for sure.

It wasn't all night-time mayhem. Sometimes on our sunny days off work we used to go to the Hampstead Women's Pond - I really loved it up there. It was awkward to get to when we didn't have any transport of our own but it felt like paradise to me. I wasn't used to being in such beautiful scenic places. Having been brought up on a council estate in Manchester we rarely got to see such natural beauty like the Women's Pond. As small an area as it was, I relished in its peace and tranquility. Not forgetting all the half-naked bathers of course. Only joking! I loved the freedom of women being able to lie naked, bare their breasts and just chill out without the worry of some pervy bloke nearby. You still used to get blokes in the bushes perving on us. Men can be so pathetic but even so, most of the time it was just wonderful.

We had an Auntie in Acton in West London, who was disabled and lived on her own. Not nearly enough times we would meet up with her at Kew Gardens in West London, on a Sunday afternoon. I loved Kew Gardens; again, I'd never been to places like that. Lancaster had a few nice scenic places to go to, but when you're young you're not really that interested. Sometimes we'd call to her flat in Acton for our tea, we'd chat and have a nice time. She'd lived with us for about five years when we were kids in Manchester, so we were quite close to her really. I always felt guilty that we hardly ever went over to see her, maybe only once every six weeks or so, as she absolutely loved us going over. What really made it so awful was that there was a massive gay club called Lemons on every Friday night which we went to for weeks on end. And guess where is was? Yes, Acton. We had no trouble getting to and from there of course, even though it would be 2 or 3 in the morning before we'd leave to get all the way back home. It hurts me just to think about all the guilt, of not going to see my poor old lonely, disabled Auntie. It was a cracking club though, Lemons, what an atmosphere with Sylvester's record blaring out, 'You make me feel, mighty real.' Fantastic.

We had an old string hammock in our sparse back garden. One morning coming off a night shift from the hospital, I thought seeing as it was such a beautiful day, I would go to bed in the hammock. I'd finished my last shift of nights, so what better way to celebrate then resting in a lovely soft hammock with fresh air and sunshine. As usual after coming off a night shift I slept like a log. I woke up about 12.30 midday with one side of my face bright red. My light skin couldn't take much of the strong sun at the best of times, never mind being asleep in the midday sun. I felt really rough and looked insane. It wouldn't have been so bad if it was both sides of my face and that night we were going to a newly opened women's bar. It was a Monday so we weren't expecting a wild night really. Kate and I were slightly back on together at the time, by a very thin thread, I might add. She liked the security and friendship, I think, of being round Hannah and me, so she came with us as did Vicky, Alex and Gemma.

Despite putting loads of cream on my burnt face it was still bright red. I felt rough, partly from my long shift of nights as well as the sunburn. It was a nice bar. The women who ran it were very welcoming of us. As the night went on I noticed one woman in particular who couldn't keep her eyes off Kate - she kept moving nearer and nearer to her. I was getting more and more drunk the nearer she got. I was really giving her the evil eye. How much more of anything could I take, right under my fucking nose again? The woman was quite a bit older than me and Kate and obviously a bit thick to have such a big death wish. I'd never been violent to anyone but I was getting so angry I probably looked like I could kill. Hannah was getting very stressed out by me. She said I looked absolutely bonkers, with my bright red, half-burnt face and dark drunkenness towards Kate and this woman. Kate didn't speak to the woman but I knew something was going on. Hannah managed to talk me round and the woman's friend came to sit at the bar stool next to me after I'd calmed down a bit. She was trying to chat me up. It was probably a ploy to distract me while her mate stole my love. We eventually left with everybody unscathed, well almost. I was very upset really by the whole day and night. I'd been so thrilled that Kate was coming for a night out with me as she hardly ever did that anymore. She'd turn up in the pub quite often, but not especially to see me.

The following week, after another stint of nights, I arrived home in the morning to find Kate in my bed. I was absolutely thrilled. She'd avoided me like mad since that night, and as usual had said it was a bad idea for us to carry on seeing each other. Yet here she now was in my bed - what joy. I quickly got undressed so I could get in bed with her, but before I could get in she went all weird and shot out of the bed. As usual, I couldn't work out what was up with her – who did ever know what went on inside her mind? She left hurriedly and I fell asleep. That evening Hannah told me that Kate had been in the Jube with the woman from the bar on Monday and that she'd let them sleep in my bed, 'cos they had nowhere else to sleep. I felt sick. I couldn't get so mad with Hannah, she was always getting caught in the middle of me and Kate. She was still only 18 and didn't have the worldly knowledge to say no to Kate. I was very down yet again by it all.

But we made some cracking friends, two of whom were Tracy and Clare. What a laugh we always had with them. They were a couple and lived in a nice flat in Blackheath. They were at our house every weekend and used to stay over. It was funny because they had a lovely posh flat, yet they preferred to stay in our squat - freezing cold in the winter, no hot water and an outside bog. They were both from the North as well, although I think they met down here. They had a friend of theirs called Sasha living with them for a while. We used to pretend that me, Gemma and Hannah were a family - me the Dad, Gemma the mum and Hannah our kid, just for a laugh. We also pretended that Clare, Tracy and Sasha were our posh relatives - Clare the Dad, Tracy the Mum and Sasha the kid. We were called the 'commons' because we lived in a scruffy house in a rough area, and they were called the 'poshies' because Blackheath was a posh area and they had a nice flat. We had so much fun play acting with our different roles and it kept us amused for hours. I think we decided that Mrs Poshie (Tracy) was my sister, who had done well for herself by marrying Clare and going to live in Blackheath, and that she couldn't stay away from her rough roots. That's why she was over in Stepney the whole time. We would often all be crying laughing with the fun we had.

Even the first time we met them was hilarious. We'd gone up to a women's conference in Birmingham for the weekend with Vicky and Alex and a few others. On the Saturday night there was a social which was the only reason we'd gone to the conference - we just wanted to meet new women and have a good time. To get upstairs to the social we had to walk through a bar, which turned out to be very crowded and very rough. As we were standing together in the bar, trying to work out where the entrance was for the upstairs, a big gang of really nasty looking men were standing right next to us looking like they wanted to kill us. They were drunk and getting more and more threatening by the second. I could see Hannah shitting herself though the other women didn't seem as aware of it as we were (not used to rough places like us maybe). What looked like the ring leader, the tallest out of them and the cockiest looking, came right up to my face and asked me which borstal I'd been in. I smiled and looked him right in the eye and said the name of the borstal in Manchester.

'Risley. Why, do you know it?' I said, smiling like I really had been in a borstal and he was my mate also from a borstal, otherwise why would he ask me? Oh and by the way mister ringleader thug, if I am an ex-borstal person then see this in my eyes - I might have a big fuck-off knife in my pocket and I'm not afraid to use it, so keep your fucking distance. We left quite casually to go upstairs, Hannah and I keeping our cool, the rest of our group oblivious to these really terrifying events. We felt a bit safer upstairs in the disco away from all that.

After the social we gathered outside to see where else we could go to. Suddenly there was a scuffle right next to us.

'Quick there's a man beating up a woman,' we heard somebody say.

Hannah and I were pissed by now. With all that nastiness from those men earlier, people were more vigilant, so a few of us jumped into the scuffle to try and sort things out. It was dark so you couldn't see what the hell was going on. People seemed to be falling about the place and throwing the odd drunken feeble punches around. A woman punched me, not very hard in the face through the mayhem. It was all a bit bonkers really. Nobody seemed to know what was happening so we left them to it, seeing as there didn't actually appear to be any real danger. The next day we were in the pub at lunchtime and we could see a group of women nearby.

'Ere that's that woman who punched me in the face last night', I said to Hannah, looking over at the group. They smiled and nodded over at us. We ended up all chatting to each other and it turned out that it was Clare who had punched me in the face, not deliberately of course. Like everyone else, she was pissed and just doing what she thought was best by throwing punches around. It turned out to be a massive misunderstanding. There was no bloke attacking a woman at all, just a man walking past. He got embroiled in the fight as well by default - I think he got on the end of the most punches. We thought it was the funniest thing ever that Clare had hit me - what a way to make friends with people. Sadly though, a woman was punched in the eye by one of a group of men after we left to go upstairs, probably by one of the thugs who'd started on us. We didn't find out till later that day. She had a massive shiner, poor thing.

I was quite tough really when I was a small kid as there was always some bastard bully boy or another trying to kick my head in, so I was well used to defending myself. I was tall and quite strong. One time we were in the Jube and this arsehole man decided he wanted to cause some trouble with some of our lot who were playing pool on the table near to me. As usual, he started a dispute over whose turn it was next, this was common practice to start a fight. It was bad enough women playing pool as it was, but for those women to be lesbians on top of that was criminal. When any woman got homophobic aggression towards them, they would always look to me for protection or to try and sort it out somehow, which I always did. This time I was terrified, like most times I suppose. He was saying that his game was up next, knowing damn well like everybody else that it wasn't - it was one of the women's games. I told the woman that when her game was up I'd put the money in and play the game with her. It was obvious to the arsehole that we were doing this deliberately to join forces against him. I'd been playing on another table and she'd been sat with somebody else ready to play them. He had been itching for a fight as soon as he came in the pub. As usual, he wasn't local. All the local men knew us and weren't threatened by us. Anyway, I walked over to pick the money up off the table and put it into the pool table. He stood up like he wanted my blood. As I was bending down to put the balls up onto the table, I was shaking with fear so much inside I could hardly breathe. The fear was so massive it had almost completely taken over me. I felt sick. Then all of a sudden I got really angry that someone had dared to make me feel so terrified. As I rose up to put the last ball on the table, the huge fear had shifted over into absolute anger. Strangely all the feelings were the same - shaking like a leaf, hardly able to breathe, feeling sick. How dare he! I was blazing. I wanted his blood. I set the game up and we played. He never said a dickey bird. From that moment on, after my alchemy moment of turning fear into anger, no bastard got the better of me.

That one incident put me in good stead for any future aggro that was part and parcel of being an out lesbian. One time when I kept me nerve well was when Penny and one of her mates came knocking on our front door to tell me there was trouble in the B.P. and some of the women were still in there. I went around to find four villainous, pissed-looking blokes who had taken possession of the bar with a small group of dykes sitting together at a table. The landlord and landlady, who must've been in their late 50s or early 60s, were behind the bar looking terrified and there was no one else in the pub. The landlord was usually quite cocky, but not tonight.

The one who looked like the leader of the villains started to walk behind the bar. The landlord and landlady barely even looked up at him, they just kept their heads low.

'This is my pub, this is,' the gang master said leaning forward over the bar. He then got a big bag of money and emptied it out on the bar - there were wads of notes held together all over the bar. Some of the other gangsters were laughing; one didn't look pleased at all.

'Right, one for you and one for you', Mr Gang master said putting a wad of notes into different piles and laughing. It was very intimidating behavior, like he was saying 'what you gonna do about me', obviously dishing out booty from a robbery of some kind. The landlady's face looked grey with fright. I always used to look people in the eye no matter what, and must've been doing the same with him. He probably wasn't getting enough of a reaction from everyone else, seeing as it was only his cronies that dared look at him, apart from me that is. I suppose I was a bit intrigued by his brass neck really - who the hell would dare to do that? He looked at me and said, 'You're scared of me, aren't you?'

'No, I'm not', I said.

I really wasn't, at this point. I was so used to violent behavior. A part of me thought, you can't threaten me any more than I've been threatened in the past. This philosophy, on top of the bastard at the pool table scenario, helped me get through this predicament now in the B.P. I didn't stay long after this. It all happened very quickly and before I knew it, he just laughed, necked his drink, gathered the stash of money up and left with all his cronies. The women could then leave the pub freely, without fear of attack from the gangster thugs.

Stepney seemed like the center of the lesbian universe. Women came from not only all over London and the rest of England, but also from all over the world. There was a great social scene - there'd be parties all the time in one of the many lesbian squats of the area, plenty of pool to be played in the pubs and best of all, lots of hot women to fancy.

One such hot woman was Ella, a tall, dark, stunningly beautiful woman who I saw sitting in the garden at number 34 talking to Vicky and Alex. She was with another woman, her girlfriend I found out later. I was star struck when I first feasted my eyes on her. I thought she'd never even give me the time of day, seeing as she looked like she'd just stepped off the cover of *Vogue* magazine and besides, she had a girlfriend. I fancied her rotten. I met her a few times after that down the pub with everyone else. She lived nearby and was usually in without her girlfriend. It was only a matter of time before we finally got into bed. Phew, how hot was she. She was tall like me and every inch one sexy bitch. I couldn't believe my luck.

Hannah and I had become pals with some of the women from the various lesbian theatre groups that hung around the Stepney social scene. One of the women, Maddy, was always thrilled to see me. We used to go out together in the daytime quite a bit. I fancied her like mad as soon as I'd seen her, before I'd met Ella. Maddy lived with her girlfriend and was truly drop dead gorgeous. Everywhere we went, people swooned over her. She was very posh and played a lot of leading roles in women's theatre. I got on well with Robyn, her girlfriend, and she didn't seem bothered that Maddy was all over me all the time, and that we went out together to places like Regent's Park and Kew Gardens.

Gemma made me laugh - she couldn't get over the fact that someone like Maddy had shown an interest in me. She was horrified that we went out on daytime dates to the park.

'You don't take a woman like Maddy out to the park', she said, despairing of me.

I just smiled, slightly annoyed at her pretentiousness and didn't say anything. Maddy knew that Kate was sometimes my girlfriend. She wasn't bothered and neither was Kate about her. Mind you, Kate would have trouble being bothered though, with her track record of going off the rails since we moved down to London. Maddy was very put out, however, when she found out I was shagging Ella. Maddy and I hadn't actually had sex at this point - we just went out on these beautiful, truly romantic daytime dates. I never really liked to make a move on anybody. I suppose I thought if they wanted me then they would make a move on me. I was surprised at Maddy's strong reaction to me seeing Ella, especially as she was with Robyn and I was still seeing Kate, on and off. Maybe it was because Ella was new and Maddy had always had people making a move on her. I told her it made no difference to me and her whatsoever, and that I could still sleep with other people if I wanted. She was pleased with that.

Ella and I had only been seeing each other for a few weeks before Kate started trying to beguile me. I was annoyed with her at first for trying to mess my life up again but it was no time at all before she was back in my bed. One morning the bed was still warm from Ella leaving when Kate got back in with me. Another time, we were walking down the street nearby, holding hands and who should be walking towards us but Ella. I immediately went to let go of Kate's hand, but she wouldn't let me and hung on to my hand. Poor Ella had the humiliation of having to stand there and make conversation with me. I felt really humiliated as well. I couldn't cope with seeing both of them at the same time so Ella and I fizzled out, what more or less felt like there and then. My nerves couldn't take it really. I liked Ella as well. She'd finished with her girlfriend when she started seeing me and now look what had happened.

More Speed, More Chaste

It was not surprising that Kate hated living in
the nurses' home, so it wasn't long until she
decided that she had to move out. She asked Amy
and Teresa from number 26 whether she could
move in with them; they said yes, so here she was
living on our street. It didn't make a massive
difference to me really, 'cos I knew that even
though we had split up she'd always be around the
area somewhere or other. But it turned out that it
really did make a difference after a couple of
months, when she told me that she and Teresa,
Amy's girlfriend no less, were having an affair
behind Amy's back. Kate made it clear that I
wasn't allowed to tell anybody. We weren't
together at the time, but nonetheless I was still in
love with her and very upset by it. I hated the
deception of it all and I really resented having to
protect that ugly fuck Teresa, keeping her sordid
affair secret from everybody so Amy didn't find
out. Never mind my nose being rubbed in, having
the prospect of running into Kate anytime day or
night, I felt soiled by it. I didn't even tell Hannah.

Kate still used to come out for sessions at the
pub or to parties with me and Hannah on a regular
basis, especially since she was now officially our

neighbor. One memorable occasion was when Jill, a friend of mine from Lancaster who had moved across the Pennines to Bradford in Yorkshire, came down to visit. We went over to Brixton in the daytime, to visit a mutual friend of ours. Jessie was an important person to all of us – me, Hannah and Jill – but we had some concerns about where she was living and – especially – who she was living with. Jessie was a black woman sharing space with a bunch of white women; they didn't like it when we were there smoking dope after we'd been in the pub at dinner time, or if we were drinking cans of beer and generally having a good time. We'd had enough of the mind games, so the group of us agreed to go over to some other mates of Jessie's in Hackney to carry on our party.

We knew Jessie's mates a bit; they loved it that we turned up out of the blue to party and immediately sent out to the off-licence for more supplies. Inevitably this didn't include any food; by about eight o'clock we were hanging drunk and stoned out of our heads. Then Jill, my visitor and so-called friend, suddenly started to ask me personal questions, including quizzing me about whether I was still involved with Kate. I wouldn't give her a straight answer; Kate was in the room and it was the biggest no-go area in the world. But Jill was as macho as most macho men are, and about as subtle and as sensitive as a sodding sledgehammer. She wouldn't let it go, so I told her, 'No, we're not together', which we weren't on that precise day.

I clammed up and felt myself sinking into the old humiliating shit. I tried not to let it show, doing my best to seem buoyant at this very pissed-up soiree. The can of worms that had long since turned into a barrel of worms had cracked open and those worms were starting to wriggle around in the pit of my stomach. As usual I tried to ignore the pain and carry on with my life. I liked being with Jessie and her friends, they were good craic.

The next thing I knew Jessie came back into the room. She always called me Cecilia instead of Cecily, and sat down across the room from me, looked over and said, 'Cecilia, Jill's having it off with your wife downstairs'.

I slowly looked around the room to see that the two of them weren't in sight and gradually got to my feet to go downstairs. As I walked into the living room they were both on the couch, fully clothed but kissing. Jill saw me, jumped up and started whimpering about how sorry she was. I didn't even look at her; she shot out of the room, a pathetic ugly streak of misery. Meanwhile, Kate just sat there doing her usual act of saying and doing absolutely fuck all, apart from turning my heart to dust. This was the lowest yet, to get off with one of my supposed best friends while I was upstairs. I walked over to her and got hold of either side of her waistcoat while she was still sat on the couch and pulled her up towards me. A couple of her buttons came undone.

'Why do you keep doing this to me?' I asked her, face to face and still holding onto her waistcoat. 'How much lower do ya think I can go? I can't go any further'.

I wasn't shouting but I was gripping onto her clothes very tightly and holding her very close to my face. I desperately wanted her to stop treating me like this, hurting and humiliating me so much. I was shaking, she had tears in her eyes, but once again she had nothing to say about her terrible actions. I let go of her and went back upstairs.

All was quiet as I stepped into the room.

'You shouldn't beat women up,' one of Jessie's friends said to the whole group of women.

I couldn't understand why she said this, but I wanted to leave straight away. Everything was too distorted and horrible. Hannah came outside with me to get a taxi back to Stepney and when we got into the street she suddenly turned and punched me in the face. It wasn't too hard – but this was because she was too pissed rather than because she didn't mean it. I didn't have a clue as to what was going on. Hannah wasn't violent at all – Mam brought us up to be very non-violent. Nonetheless I punched her back, not very hard either. She looked shocked and said to me, 'Don't you ever lay a finger on her again'.

I suddenly realized that she meant Kate. 'I never touched her. I grabbed hold of her waistcoat, that's all,' I said.

'Jill said you beat her up,' Hannah retorted.

'Yeah, well, I fucking didn't,' I said, annoyed at Jill. On top of everything else, now people thought I was a wife batterer. Things couldn't get any worse. Then Hannah and I laughed as we stood in the street. To think of us two of all people throwing punches at each other. We thought everything was hilarious again, like we usually did. We got back to Stepney and went straight to the Jube.

There were loads of women in the pub that night, but we just sat together at the bar, still laughing from all the madness. I told her about Kate having an affair with Teresa, the thing I wasn't meant to tell anyone; I didn't care anymore what happened. I didn't really want to socialize with the other women in the pub. I thought the word would be out in no time that I was a wife batterer, and everyone would want my blood. 'It will be my word against Kate and Jill,' I thought, 'even though Jill was out of the room at the time and, oh yeah, she's meant to be one of my best friends.' How could I forget that?

Kate turned up about an hour later, all smiles towards me, standing right next to me as she was ordering a drink at the bar. Hannah and I had drunk ourselves sober by this time and we were all ready for another session. I completely ignored Kate. It was all over, I was finally free of her. I didn't like the memory of getting hold of her by the waistcoat earlier and pulling her so her face was up against to mine. That wasn't me. I suppose when you get dragged down so low and your dignity begins to suffer, you end up being in nasty places. Most self-respecting people have to know when to pull out. Love has no meaning anymore, it just becomes a word. When I let her go, downstairs in that Hackney house, it was in both senses of the phrase.

We carried on drinking and playing pool, despite hardly being able to stand up, till the early hours of the morning. Nobody thought I was a wife batterer thank god, they knew me too well; besides, Kate was in the pub all smiles and happy towards me.

Next morning, after we had left the pub at about 2am, Lucy from number 46 came round to warn us that Amy and Teresa were on the warpath. Apparently Teresa had come round at about midnight the night before, with an iron bar, to smash my head in. What the fuck was this madness about? It turned out that someone had told them that I had beaten up Kate, maybe even Kate herself. She was with them both at the time and Teresa went ballistic and grabbed an iron bar, then set off down to my house to sort me out, for supposedly beating up one of her women. As she was about to set off Amy twigged that Teresa and Kate were up to no good and challenged them about whether they were having a clandestine relationship. After seeing Teresa's strong reaction to the accusation that I had been violent to Kate, it was glaringly obvious what was going on between them so Amy set about fighting Teresa while Kate tried to stop them. Meanwhile Hannah and I had still been quite happily drinking and playing pool in the pub, blissfully unaware of all this mayhem.

With Lucy's news we were expecting them to call round that morning for more madness. We had hours of fun planning what we'd do when they turned up. We stood in the hall. We really took the piss.

'So, you answer the door,' I said to Hannah, 'and when she sees me over your shoulder and tries to hit me with the bar, I'll duck over 'ere, swing round and punch her just like this,' I said, play acting all the movements. We screamed and screamed laughing. We even pretended to knock on the front door and talked to the imaginary Amy and Teresa – who never actually turned up after all that. The adrenaline rush of having to be ready for a fight made us high. I wasn't scared in the slightest; I suppose a part of me was very angry at their dreadful threat of violence towards me. I felt that we could've easily taken them on, iron bar or no iron bar. Hannah was terrified of fighting, but she was confident that I was strong and fast enough for both of us if need be. And I knew she would stand up for me if push came to shove; she was quite tall as well, and strong. Neither of us liked fighting at all, but we could handle ourselves if we had to.

Things changed with Kate after the all-time low of that dreadful night; I had too much self-respect to carry on living in such a horrible emotional place; my head and heart had moved on at last! It didn't bother me that she was still around the scene, nor who she got off with. I still cared about her, but I wasn't hooked into her like I used to be. When our Bernie used to come down from Lancaster to visit she would pop in to see Kate, or she would come round to ours for a cup of tea. I tried to keep a healthy distance; we'd still sleep together the odd time but I didn't get pulled into her web again.

We had a party at our house one weekend around that time, it was packed as usual. Someone persuaded me to take some speed. It made my jaw work overtime, uncomfortably so. I didn't talk that much more than usual, but I kept moving my jaw up and down and it was doing my head in. The same reaction had happened a few years earlier and I hadn't taken it since then, but stupidly I here I was again. Maddy was at this party with Robyn, her official girlfriend; we were dating at the time but still hadn't had sex. She kept dancing right into me, rubbing her body against mine, teasing me and turning me on like mad. We'd never been so overtly sexual with each other. She disappeared for about ten minutes, the next thing was that Robyn came up to me and told me that Maddy was upstairs in bed, she wasn't very well and could I go up to see her? I trotted upstairs and found her lying in bed, in the darkness. I sat on the edge of the bed for all of one second, before months of quelled passions overcame Maddy, as she pulled me towards her and at long last we kissed and dragged the clothes off each other. Sadly I couldn't get into it properly, because the speed's effect on my jaw was getting in the way of our love making, after such a long wait for her it felt like sod's law! We'd broken the spell though and carried on having sex for a couple of months after that.

It wasn't always easy being Maddy's girlfriend, in some ways I preferred it before we'd had sex. Suddenly more people who I barely knew started to want a piece of me for some weird reason. One time we came back after being out somewhere and Hannah had let Kate come round to watch telly at our house even though she must have known that I would be coming home with Maddy. I do love my sister but it has to be said that she could be a bit thick sometimes. It was very awkward being there with Kate; she just stayed pretending to watch the flickering screen while me and Maddy went to bed in the next room. Of course I couldn't have sex while she was just the other side of the curtain. Another time we were laid in bed and a fucking mouse appeared on the bedroom floor, and just stood there staring up at us. That was a surreal moment.

It wasn't meant to be, Maddy and me being together. Kate shagged Robyn at some point as well, just to make it even more mental. I really did prefer our daytime dates from before we started having sex. Ah well, I wasn't too disappointed because there was always an array of beautiful women in and around the area and I could soon distract myself with them.

One such woman was Rachel, an Australian travelling woman, who lived in a squat in Hackney with her girlfriend Toni but spent a lot of time on her own in Stepney. We got on well and used to have a good laugh. One night it seemed to be on the cards that we would get off together. There were a load of us women in the pub, and Gemma found out that I fancied Rachel. Being the prick that she sometimes was, she decided that she could easily 'pull her' if she wanted to, that I would have no chance against her. Gemma didn't even fancy Rachel, it was all a stupid macho game to her; I was really pissed off with her and just ignored her completely, as did Hannah and Rachel for that matter. Gemma gave up in the end after she'd made a complete prat of herself and went home. Kate and Clare and a couple of other people were staying over at ours that night, in the living room that was the other side of my bedroom only divided by a curtain! I had four of them listening to our every move till daylight. Not only that, but after Rachel had gone home I had to listen to a blow by blow account of what they could and could not hear. We were all in hysterics.

Clare was saying, 'I thought oh that's it, they must be going to sleep now, when I heard you being quiet, thank god for that, but then no you started again, it must've been about six o'clock this morning before we managed to get any sleep'. They all roared laughing again. I wasn't too bothered about them being there. They knew the score if you had to stay over and there were no beds free.

One time before Rachel and I got off together, she and Toni came over to ours for tea. We were having a really good laugh with them when Hannah decided to go to the toilet outside; I went downstairs to the kitchen in the basement directly underneath the living room. While Hannah was coming back from the lav she decided that she'd knock on the living room window, to say hello to Rachel and Toni. There were some doors in the kitchen that opened out onto a scummy unused little outside bit, like an open cellar. The next thing I knew there was the most unmerciful crash in the kitchen. I jumped out of my skin, and then looked through the windows of the outside doors and there was Hannah lying in a heap on the ground, moaning in agony. I got hysterical laughing; I didn't even know if the doors opened or not but I knew it was filthy in there. Rachel and Toni came running down the stairs to see what the big crash was. They'd seen her knocking on the window and then disappear. They were both doubled up laughing as well. We had to try and stop as quick as we could 'cos Hannah was obviously in agony. In my hysteria and fright from the terrible crash, I couldn't work out how to get her out from this disgusting filthy area. I went upstairs and outside to look down from where she'd fallen; I thought, 'Oh we'll have to get a rope, tie it round her and haul her up'. It never occurred to me that I could get her out through the kitchen doors. She was getting really pissed off being stuck down there in agony and was shouting at me to get her out. I came back down to the kitchen quickly and came back to my senses, and opened the doors to get her out. She'd really hurt her foot.

The next day I stayed off work to take her to Casualty, 'cos she was still in a lot of pain. They said it was a badly sprained ankle and bandaged it up then let her go. She had her arm around my shoulder all the time to be able to walk; we had got a taxi to the hospital and were trying to get one back home. We made it to the hospital entrance then stood to see if we could find one. She still had her arm around my shoulder, when suddenly I spotted one and dived over towards it, forgetting that I was Hannah's support. Of course she went flying and went over on her bad foot again, I dived back to pick her up from the floor. I felt awful, me a nurse, I should really have known better. I suppose I didn't have my nurse's head on. Anyway, we didn't have to go back in for more treatment, thank god, and after a few days Hannah went back to work.

Mam was coming to visit for the first time; she was calling in on her way to a hosteling holiday in France, with a friend's grown-up daughter. They were coming on a Friday evening and staying over at ours. We wanted everything to be perfect for the visit. However, things were far from perfect when I got home from work on the Friday afternoon, only a few hours before Mam was due to land. For quite a few months, Hannah had been seeing Ruth, a Jewish woman, who was twice her age. Although she was supposed to be with Hannah she always had a roving eye and fancied herself as some kind of super sex goddess, totally self-appointed I might add. She was another one who – despite being a hairdresser in a back-street shop – lived in a posh house and used to stay at our house all the time.

Ruth had gone up to Bradford to see some of her mates for a few days, and while she was there she got off with a mixed-race woman called Charlie. Hannah knew nothing about this and had assumed, like you would, that Ruth was still her girlfriend. The next thing she knew she was getting the bus after work at her usual stop and her usual time, when who was standing across the road from her but Ruth and this woman Charlie, in a passionate embrace for poor Hannah to see. She couldn't believe her eyes. Ruth was saying goodbye to Charlie before she went to tell Hannah it was all over between them. But she sadistically stood outside her place of work, and kissed this new woman in front of Hannah for some kind of sick pleasure. I arrived home about an hour after Hannah did, to find that Ruth didn't even have the decency to leave after Hannah had found out about the end of their relationship. She was still hanging around our house, like everything was hunky dory. She seemed to be almost reveling in the twisted attention she imagined that she was receiving. She certainly didn't get a shred of anything from me. I never even glanced at her for a split second, not once. Despite her inflated egotistical idea of her own power and importance, she couldn't have shown me a more horrible, nasty side if she'd tried.

As soon as I walked in the door and found out what had happened, I grabbed both Hannah and Gemma and we went off to the King's Arms, a pub at the end of our street that we'd hardly ever been in. I chose that pub because I knew that none of the other women in the street would be in, and creepy Ruth wouldn't think to follow us there either. The plan was just to stay for an hour, while we made sure that Hannah was going to be okay for when Mam arrived. Hannah hadn't had a girlfriend before for any length of time, so this major nasty upset was all very new to her. I told her that Ruth was shit for doing what she'd done, it was one thing sleeping with someone else, but to wait for Hannah to come out of work and stand at her bus stop, then publicly kiss the woman you've been shagging all week, this was really out of order. Anyone who did that sort of thing, I told her, wasn't worth even spitting on, she was nothing and Hannah had far better values than to be with someone who behaved so badly.

'You must stick to your strongly-held principles. If she wants to live her life in such a disgusting manner, then that woman Charlie is welcome to her. She must be like that as well to go along with all that bloody rubbish, kissing at the fuckin' bus stop. How childish is that!' I continued.

My speech seemed to be starting to work after just over an hour and two pints each. We were pleased, the mood was light again, thank god, and the timing for Mam's arrival was perfect, all that was left to do was for Hannah to make sure that Ruth got out of our house as soon as we got back home. Job well done, I thought, that is until the pub landlord came over to us with a pint of lager each on the house. We couldn't work out why he'd done this, we barely knew him. We thanked him, drank the beer on empty stomachs and were half pissed before we'd finished, he bought another round of drinks over. He was chatting away to everyone in the pub, this quite old, small, white-haired East End man. I'd never have taken him to be so friendly when I'd called in the odd time in the past. His wife was Italian and younger than him, she was a bit wild looking and people seemed a bit nervous of her. I don't know what was going on that evening, we weren't used to people being nice to us, apart from Bill, the Jube landlord, and that seemed an extreme one-off. Two more free pints later and we staggered out of the pub. I was shocked when the fresh air hit me in the face, how the hell are we going to be able to entertain Mam now I thought. I could've just gone home and crashed out there and then.

We somehow managed to get a meal together for our visitors. In the drunken mayhem Hannah never asked Ruth to leave, or if she did then Ruth ignored her. We'd already arranged earlier in the week that no girlfriends were allowed to stay while Mam was visiting, this also included Gemma's. She wasn't bothered by this embargo; she knew we'd do the same for her if needs be. Hannah and I were out to our mother, but this was fairly recent so we weren't used to the freedom of having a girlfriend openly stay over under her gaze, hence the self-imposed embargo.

We were thrilled to see Mam; I was disappointed that we were so drunk, or drunk so early anyway; it would've been ok later. I think half the women on our street were nervous about our Mam's visit. Both Hannah and I wanted her first visit to go down well and we wanted her to feel comfortable amongst all the Lesbians. She's always been very easy going about most things, and didn't seem the slightest bit bothered that we were so drunk when she arrived, though I suppose we would've been trying to act more sober than we really were.

Everyone in the house, including stupid Ruth, came to the Jube after we'd eaten our tea. There were a few women in already, all dying to meet our Mam. After more pints of lager I fell off a bar stool and hoped to god that Mam hadn't seen me. Inside my drunken stupor I was mortified by my own behavior, knowing that Mam must've seen me falling off the stool. Then Kate turned up at the pub, despite me asking her to stay away; but Mam loved Kate so it was okay. Gemma's girlfriend turned up on her motorbike, just for the one drink. She said she wouldn't stay over, but one drink turned into two then three. All the while Ruth showed no signs of leaving. The whole troupe of us ended up back at the house. Gemma's girlfriend was over the limit so stayed over after all; Ruth wanted one last drop of Hannah's blood, and as usual Kate did whatever she liked and, as usual, I let her, so they both stayed over as well. So much for our girlfriend embargo. It all turned out fine though; Mam went off on her holiday to France the next day, after we'd gone to the station with her to wave her off. It couldn't have been too awful as they stayed on their way back as well, only this time we made damned sure that it wasn't such a drunken mad affair!

Even the nursing agency I worked for was run by two women who I thought were lesbians. Miss Rigby and Miss Green were in their fifties I think. As usual of that generation of lesbians one was quite butch and one quite femme. I rather fancied the femme one if I'm honest, even though she was loads older than me. I worked at quite a few different hospitals through their agency; sometimes just a for couple of days, but it could be a few weeks or months. The Jewish Hospital at Stepney, a couple of nights at the Royal Free at Hampstead, the Ear Nose & Throat at Soho, St Thomas', St Mark's on City Road between the Angel and Old Street, and last but not least also on City Road, the world-famous Moorfields Eye Hospital. Some I really hated; some I hated less. I was quite intrigued to work at Moorfields, because eyes were just about the only thing left that I hadn't nursed. Besides, I saw it as one of the biggest challenges. Out of all the various parts of the body to need medical attention, I imagined that eyes would make me the most squeamish. I was already squeamish as hell which did not work well with being a nurse. But when it came to it, I found that, strangely enough, I didn't feel any more squeamish with eyes than I did with other parts of the body. I thought that eyes represented the most human part of the body, apart from mouths, and my sense was that people always looked into each other's eyes when they spoke, or when they were attracted to each other. But in reality this is not what happens, people tend to look at each other's mouths. And it was mouths that I found the hardest to nurse, which really surprised me. I suppose the dentist association comes up the most when you think of things happening inside your mouth. But having worked in orthodontics where doctors and dentists operate on mouths, quite often under local anesthetic, it's a different story. I used to have to watch people having their gums cut into and other horrible things that I'm too squeamish to recall.

Luckily I never saw any eye operations. On one occasion a horrible thing nearly happened but I had a narrow escape. An elderly woman came in for an operation on her eye; she had a false eye and like, all patients, had to take any false eyes, teeth, legs, arms etc. off, or out, before they went to the operating theatre. This old lady had her false eye put in nine years ago. It was my job to make sure that she took her false eye out, before she went down to theatre. But when I asked her to take it out, she said she didn't know how to because she'd never had it out, since the day it was put in nine years earlier. I was horrified. Nobody had bothered to even tell her that she needed to take it out, and wash it and clean the empty eye socket, but hadn't even shown her how to do it. I didn't know how to anyway, but that wouldn't stop a lot of ward sisters making you do things that you'd never done before. Fortunately this ward sister had a human side and took it out herself. I made myself busy so I didn't have to see it. Yuk!

Working as an agency nurse in London was mostly a lot easier than working in Manchester and Lancaster, where I'd done my training. I started my training off in Salford, Manchester as a pupil nurse; it was a two-year training to become an enrolled nurse. You needed 'O' levels to do the three-year training to be a registered nurse (the ones who could get promotion and give people heavy-duty medication). People at my school hardly ever got an 'O' level, so I had to do the 'cheap labor' training route. I transferred to Lancaster half way through because I hated Salford so much, and absolutely adored Lancaster.

After working in such a deprived area as Salford, I thought I'd seen and nursed just about everything, until I transferred to Lancaster. I'd only been on the female and children's surgical ward for a few weeks before I had to go on nights. During the day it was like a mad house, it was so busy. There would be two ward sisters, a staff nurse, two student nurses, a pupil nurse and an auxiliary nurse; at night it was just me and an auxiliary nurse who was restricted in what she could and couldn't do. It was the only female and kids' surgical ward for 20 miles south and 80 miles north. We had any accidents on the M6 motorway coming into us, a big university, a holiday camp, the Lake District, the Yorkshire Dales, schools, colleges, you name it; we were permanently inundated with emergency admissions day and night. One particularly bad night I saw the blue light of an ambulance pull up outside, and I hoped and prayed that it was a man and not a woman, because I literally didn't have a split second to spare to take in another patient. A ward packed to the seams with people whose lives depended on me. I was only 19 as well. I didn't dare leave the ward to go for a meal break to the canteen, the auxiliary nurse would've been on her own; it was bad enough me being in charge with what little training I had, never mind someone with no training whatsoever.

When I used to get home and into bed after a twelve-hour night shift, I would be asleep before my head hit the pillow every time. I'd get up after eight hours sleep, have my tea then fall asleep on the couch till it was time to go back to the frantic speed of the night shift. Even in the daytime basic hygiene was severely neglected because it was so busy; women died after routine operations because of the dreadful unhygienic conditions. One old lady had been in for six weeks, she'd been very ill and had terrible high temperatures so sweated a lot. One day I asked her if she'd like a bed bath, she said she'd love one because she'd not had a wash for six weeks.

I packed in nursing as soon as I qualified, there was so much I hated about it. I had to go back after a year so that I had some money coming in when I moved to London. I was surprised (after I'd got away from horrible Miss Springham at the Westminster Hospital, that is) how different most of the hierarchy treated me. In the North, they seemed to think that they could speak to you like you were dirt. There were still a few in London who thought they could behave like this, but mostly they were reasonably nice to me.

I was very skilled and nothing really phased me after my time in Salford and Lancaster. One time, on one of the wards in St Thomas', I came across a male patient who had been in an accident. He was very old-school in his outlook. He must've been in his 50s and wouldn't have it that he was ill as a result of his accident. All he wanted to do was get back to work. When I came on duty, the ward sister said in her daily report that they had more or less given up on him, because not only had he refused treatment, but he also was refusing food and much more dangerously, any fluids. His grown-up sons were very worried about him; there didn't seem to be a wife in the picture. Anyway, he wouldn't speak to anyone, and if he could've walked, he'd have been long gone out of hospital. He was starting to get confused from his lack of fluids. I thought, 'Right matey we'll soon see about you.' Although I hadn't actually met him, I felt sure that I could get him to drink. Before I went into his side ward, I checked what was in the ward fridge and noticed two bottles of beer. The ward sister did say that he could drink anything, so I put my plan into action.

Knowing that quite a few older patients didn't always feel that young nurses and doctors were old enough to look after them properly, particularly when they were very ill, I put my shoulders back, chest out and walked into the side ward. Without saying a word or hardly looking the awkward old bugger in the eye, I instead walked around the room slowly and deliberately. He looked up at me in the silence, like he was going to take me seriously. I knew I'd got him, just by that one look.

'There's a lot of young people in this place,' I heard him mutter.

I walked to the end of his bed and lifted off his charts that were clipped to the bed, pretending to read them.

'Yes, there are a lot of young people working here, they do a good job 'an all,' I said, still not looking at him and still pretending to read the charts. I put them down and looked straight at him, saying, 'You know, there are a lot of men in here,' nodding towards the main ward door, 'who are in with the same thing as you, some of them worse. None of them can get back to work neither,' I said, shaking my head. He looked surprised, he was so busy fretting about his own business and the desperate urge to get back to work, that he hadn't taken notice of anything else. Being in the side ward compounded his isolation, maybe. As soon as I included other men in the picture, his whole attitude changed completely.

Not only were there other men in the same boat as him just beyond that door, but some of them were more ill than he was. They weren't really, as he was so ill solely because he wouldn't drink, otherwise he would have been far better. His strong male ego, work ethic, whatever, was literally killing him and here I was, an Angel of Mercy.

'I didn't know there were other men here,' he said.

'Yeah there's a ward full of them,' I said smiling at him. He looked pleased through his slight confusion. 'I tell you what,' I said, pausing, "I've got a couple of bottles of beer in the fridge out here. How d'ya fancy one? All the other men have had one.'

'Have they?' he asked.

'Yeah, I'll go and get you a nice glass and pour you one,' I said, not waiting for him to say yes or no.

He weakly smiled up at me. I brought the beer and the glass back into the room with the beer half poured already. I poured a bit more in, in front of him so that he could see how nice and refreshing it looked.

'Wow, look at that, doesn't that look good?' I said, staring at the beer.

'Yeah it does,' he said, licking his lips as though he had been in the desert for six months. I had to help him get it to his mouth and stayed, with him until he drank the whole glass.

With being in the nurse pool, I was on a different ward each day, so it wasn't until a couple of weeks later that I returned to that ward. When I walked into the ward office for the ward report at the beginning of each shift, I was really surprised by the reception I got from the ward sister, who was sat at her desk with all the other nurses sitting around her.

'Oh look, it's Nurse Holland, the only person in the whole hospital who could get Mr Blah Blah to take a drink. Well done.' She started to clap, and all the other nurses smiled and one or two clapped as well. I was really shocked by all this attention and didn't even know that she knew my name. I just did me job and went home.

When I saw the patient in question later, he was sat up in bed and looked very well and sane. When he saw me he looked a bit shocked, almost like he was about to slip back into that place where I had found him before, so I just left the room and didn't go back in again.

At the end of my first year in London, the daily grind and conventionality of being a nurse for so bloody long had forced me to look for another job and to finally leave the fucked-up face of nursing once and for all.

Two Dopey Coppers Are After Us

I'd quite fancied being a carpenter and had heard that Newham Council were taking on, and training, female carpenters. But then the same person told me the opposite, that they weren't looking for any more female trainees. I later found out that they actually were still taking women on, but by then it was too late for me as I had already got a new job: I was now a gardener for Hackney Council.

Although I was a bit disappointed that I couldn't train as a carpenter, it was a great change. What a massive difference it was to be a gardener instead of a horrible nurse. I got paid £20 a week more, there were no shifts and no nights, I finished early on a Friday. There was no more weekend working and no responsibilities whatsoever. I was looking after the living instead of the dying. My workwear couldn't have been more different either from tight stiff collars, aprons and hats to blue overalls, a loose buttoned jacket and steel capped boots. Shorts in the summer, if I fancied, and I could get dirt all over me if needs be rather than having to be a clean and sterile nurse. Plenty of fresh air and a totally relaxed atmosphere. As we Lancashire people say, I was 'made up', finally getting away from being a nurse. I loved being a gardener.

I suddenly found myself in a very male environment. I wasn't used to this at all really, but it made a change and I quite enjoyed the difference. It wasn't just them being men that was so different - they were all working class as well. Most of the women who were on the lesbian scene were middle class, apart from the odd few. Because middle class culture is dominant, it felt like there were a lot more middle-class women in my life than there probably were.

For a very short while, Hannah and I both had girlfriends called Christine and they were friends with each other. They were both very posh which didn't really bother me, except for one time in a car when I was so angry with them that I was put off spending any time with the four of us again. Hannah's Christine, Christine F we'll call her, was driving with me, Hannah and the other Christine as passengers, over Westminster Bridge. Those three didn't know which way to go. The Christines kept saying, 'Oh, I don't know if it's this way or that way'.

I knew exactly which way it was, and kept telling them over and over, but they just completely ignored me like I was invisible. I felt so humiliated. I just wanted them to stop the car and let me out. If I'd been as posh as them they'd have been all over me and taken my directions seriously. From that day on I never spent any time alone with the four of us again.

The Christine that I was with was only a brief fling anyway. She asked me once how I could have gone out with Maddy when she was so posh. 'You all sound really posh to me,' I said.

'Maddy's much posher than me,' she replied.

I really hadn't noticed any difference between the two of their accents. I did know that Maddy wouldn't have dreamed of ignoring what I was saying in the car that day. She would've been as horrified as I was at their ignorance towards me.

I was forever getting people speaking to me like shit, or completely ignoring me like they had done in the car that day. Quite often I'd arrive out somewhere and be laughing and joking and people would ask me if I was drunk. At first I was a bit puzzled as to why they thought that I was drunk when I'd have only had a few sips of my drink. I soon began to realize that they thought I had to be drunk to be having such a good time, that I couldn't possibly be happy and laughing out loud if I wasn't drunk. After all, I was a working-class northerner. Occasionally I heard of someone asking other people about me and I'd think, 'Aye aye, I know what she's after!' If I fancied them, I'd smile at them the next time I saw them, sending a look for them to come and get me if they really wanted me. I could see women hooked in before I'd even given them my seductive smiles. More often than not, nothing ever came of those women, mostly I think because they didn't know how to communicate with me. They'd be embarrassed even, as well as not wanting to have sex with 'someone like me'. I got to recognize women like that fairly quickly, and as soon as I saw the shock in their eyes after I'd opened my mouth, I would turn and walk away. It made me laugh when I'd see them out sometime in the future and I would be with someone far posher and quite often prettier than they were. I could see their confused thoughts written all over their faces.

There was only one other female gardener, called Jackie. She was Cockney, about twelve years older than me and I really liked her a lot. She was a dyke as well. The gardeners were separated into different work groups - there were the ones inside the park and others on the outside, who worked on nearby housing estates. The ones on the outside were divided off into gangs of three. I was on the outside in one of these gangs. Of the three workers in each gang, one was the charge hand who sorted all the work out that we had to do. The buzz of being in touch with the earth was fantastic, even though it was only housing estates. My chargehand Jim was about the only bloke in the whole borough of Hackney who actually cared about doing a good job. We worked on a bonus scheme and every week our gang got the highest bonus in the whole of Hackney. All the stories I'd heard about council workers skiving off all the time were true, only it was ten times worse than I could have imagined. Work was a dirty word amongst council workers.

Although Hackney is quite near to Stepney as the crow flies I still had to get two buses meaning that I had to get up at a quarter to six every morning. The chance came up of buying two obviously knocked-off (stolen) racing bikes from a bloke at work - one for me, one for Hannah. We couldn't have afforded bikes if we didn't get knock-offs. It was such a thrill to cycle to work every day. I got it down to two and a half miles in thirteen minutes. It felt like all I had to do was sit on the bike, while I was still half asleep, and the next thing I knew I had arrived at work. How good was that? So much better than those two buses. When I'd get off the bike I would be all fresh and ready for the day's work. At least two days a week even us, the highest bonus gang, would skive off for the day once we had clocked in at 7:30am. I used to cycle home and go back to bed. Sometimes I would have a girlfriend still there from the night before. It made me laugh when I had sex with them as I used to think that Hackney council were paying me to have sex. I liked that idea.

Occasionally in winter I'd put my overalls on over my pajamas, knowing that I'd be back home and in bed within the hour. The days I did stay all day we would go to the pub for about two hours at dinner time, sometimes longer. A lot of the men liked pool so we would meet up and play for hours at a time. I didn't get any grief from the men, even when I beat them at pool. It made me laugh the way some of them acted around women. The whole atmosphere of the Boffy (rest room) would change the second me or Jackie would walk in. It was like the men had never seen a woman before, never mind that I was in overalls and steel capped boots. Maybe it was also because Jackie and I brought a happy feeling in with us. Gardeners can sometimes be a bit depressive. Having a lot of time on your own to think can be hard for some people, and there is plenty of time to think when you're gardening. It was such a wonderful change for me though, after being trapped inside hospitals for days and nights. I realized that the freedom of not having to think about anything, not having to worry about a patient and whether they would die on me or not, was a great relief.

Some of the housing estates were very rough. We had to go in threes to particularly rough places for our own safety. The Haggerston estate was about the worst one. I was cutting the edge of a lawn one day with my edging sheers, when all of a sudden somebody chucked a dirty, shitty baby's nappy out of an upstairs window, missing me by inches. It was gross. Another time I could hear a terrible commotion coming from the outside of a third-floor flat. I looked up to see a really small, but wide, West Indian woman roaring and shouting so loudly that everyone walking past through the estate stopped to look at her. The next thing I knew, she had picked up a washing machine and was lifting it above her head. She let out a massive roar and threw it down over the balcony. It crashed down onto the footpath at the bottom. And there was me fretting about a shitty nappy hitting me.

I liked Hackney. There was a much wider range of people there than there was in Stepney. For a kick off, there were Irish people living on the estates where I worked. One day I was just standing there hoeing over a flower bed when I heard a man's voice behind me say in an Irish accent, 'What part are you from?'.

Before I turned around, I knew exactly what he meant. It was a common phrase amongst Irish people that I had heard many a person say to my Mam and Dad. 'What part of Ireland are you from?' is what he meant, and 'Is it near the place I'm from?'. It was such a massive compliment to me, to have someone know that I was Irish without me even opening my mouth and speaking in a Northern English accent. I did open my mouth to tell him where both my Mam and Dad were from and he never batted an eyelid at my English accent. In an Irish person's eye I have very definite Irish blood running throughout my veins. Anyone else wouldn't have a clue about my Irish good looks and modesty of course!

I soon came to realize there were people from all over the world living round and about. Because of my Irish upbringing and my strong identity as a woman from the North of England, I was always chatting with whoever would chat back to me, so consequently I'd quite often be in people's houses for a cup of tea for five minutes in between mowing lawns outside. One Jamaican woman was thrilled that I worked on her estate, because I improved the quality of the whole area by always doing a thorough job. That's what she told me herself. To me it was just normal, but no one else had ever bothered before. I would rather work while I was there and get job satisfaction than skive off like everyone else. Some of the other gardeners thought that the reason I worked harder than them was because I was northern. When I say hard, it wasn't hard, not to me, though compared to them it definitely was. Another bloke in my gang, not the charge hand, was also northern and he also worked a lot harder than all of them, which still wasn't that hard.

A lot of the time people mistook me for a man at first, being tall and doing a man's job in men's overalls and boots, until that is, they started chatting to me. One day I was doing a bit of lawn edging when this young, mixed race man walked past me. He was very handsome in a slightly feminine way. As usual I smiled up at him, like I did with everyone who walked past. He didn't smile back, but stared deep into my eyes. I just looked back at him and continued to smile. He stopped walking and carried on looking at me. I thought he was gay and that he knew I was as well but maybe he just wanted a chat. It must have been hard being gay on one of these estates, especially if you were black as well. All these thoughts were going through my head. He carried on looking at me, straight into my eyes and I carried on looking at him straight in his eyes and smiling away at my black gay brother. He was my black gay brother, but unfortunately, he thought I was his white gay brother! Or potential lover more like. He was quite put out and couldn't understand why I wouldn't go and have sex with him in his flat nearby. I must've given him the green light with my eye contact and easy body language. The only word I actually said to him was 'No,' so he probably to this day still thinks that I was a man.

Parts of London's East End had a strong National Front presence, none more so than London Fields, the park where I was based. The female playground attendant in the park told me of how she still lived in fear after a massive running battle between the National Front, in the flats on one side of the park, and a large group of people who were against them on the other side. She said they charged at each other with sticks and bricks, both sides meeting up to have a pitched battle in her actual playground with her locked inside a room, frightened for her life. Apparently this had only happened the previous summer. I was always nervous of a big NF presence, me looking like an obvious out lesbian made me a sitting target. After that Asian man in our street almost got stabbed to death, I never quite took my liberty for granted in the same way again.

Bethnal Green Road had an NF pub on it called the Blade Bone - what a horrible name for a pub - and I crossed over that road at least twice a day. We had an NF member working at our park. I was very put out by it at first, but Jackie said not to worry because it's common knowledge that if someone is in the NF they've always got something wrong with them. They're not quite the full shilling and nobody takes them or their views very seriously. This was definitely true of that man who worked at our place. A few of us were down Brick Lane Market one Sunday morning when we spotted a group of about three NF members standing behind a placard selling their racist rag. Hannah was really terrified to have seen them and I was a bit nervous as well but the other women weren't that bothered. One of these NF men started to shout some fascist slogan, probably because he saw us approaching.

'No left wing lesbism!' he shouted, to which we all burst out laughing. He looked really embarrassed and ran from his soap box to hide with the others. I thought aye, it's about right what Jackie said - they're a bunch of pathetic no hopers.

I was in a blaze of a bad mood one day. I can't remember why, but I was really, really mad about something or other. Anyway, I was sitting in our front room on my own and glaring towards the window, when all of a sudden a fuckin' young skinhead's face appeared right up at the glass of the window. He was grinning like he'd come for trouble. He must've been about fifteen or sixteen. He couldn't have picked a better day as far as I was concerned, 'cos I already wanted somebody's blood, the mood I was in. The second I saw him I jumped out of my chair like some raving lunatic. I shot out of the front door wanting to kill him for daring to even think about intimidating us, never mind doing what he'd just done. Of course, in the few seconds it had taken me to get outside the front door, he'd vanished. We never had any more trouble from the likes of him after that in our street.

People had told me to be careful about removing fascist propaganda stickers that were sometimes stuck up on walls, public notice boards and that sort of place. They said that the NF would put razor blades under the stickers so if people removed them, they would cut themselves. I found it really hard to believe that anyone could be so sadistic. Once while I was at work on one of the estates on a pouring wet day, I saw one of these stickers and, because it was soaking wet from the rain, I could clearly see a razor blade underneath it. What a horrible, nasty shock I got just to see it. I managed to get it off the wall easy though, as it was so wet and the blade clear to see. Each time I saw a sticker, and usually it wasn't raining, I would feel over the surface to see if there was a razor blade underneath it. Sadly, there quite often was one.

One of the stickers was an attack on Chinese boat people who had been rescued and brought to this country. I was digging by the block of flats where the fascist people involved in the playground pitched battle lived, when I noticed one such sticker on a council notice board right next to me. Once I had checked for razor blades I did what I always did and started to remove it. Out of the blue this middle-aged man appeared from nowhere and began shouting at me. I was startled. I was always in my own little world when gardening, so he really made me jump when I just saw him, never mind for him to then start shouting.

'You can't stop people expressing themselves, it's our right to stop people coming over here!' he ranted on, with his nasty face twisted up. He had a very horrible dark presence about him. In my youth and startled state, he scared me but I said nothing back to him. Of course, when he'd gone I was mad that I hadn't tackled him about defacing council property and, as a council employee, I was going to find out which council flat he lived in and report him to the council. I couldn't have tackled him about his racist views, because I knew how violent the NF there were with loads of them just in this block of flats alone, and only one of me. But I still carried on removing their scummy stickers.

Hannah and I had some crackin' nights out, despite there being only a fraction of places to go for us compared to gay men, let alone heterosexuals. We always got the bus from the end of our street to Aldgate, a mile down the road, and then the tube. It tickled us to hear the bus conductor sometimes shouting, 'Aldgate, Aldgate, Aldgate. All change, Aldgate.' I don't know why we thought it was so funny. We hadn't heard many Cockney accents, especially not shouting out like this and telling everyone to get off the bus. If we got off the bus and he didn't shout it, Hannah would stand on the platform and shout it herself to all the passengers, then jump off as quick as she could. I would be falling over laughing. The first time we got off the tube at Bank Underground station, and we heard the loud automated voice telling us to 'Mind The Gap' we could hardly move for laughing so much. No one else could understand why we thought it was so hilariously funny.

One pub we used to go to on our nights out was the Prince Albert, down a dark back street at King's Cross. There were women's discos in the back room and the landlord was an old Irishman who gave us no grief at all. The venues for women's discos would usually only be available for a few months. Women always managed to find somewhere to go. Before I moved down to London, we used to go to the Hemingford Arms at Islington for a women's disco and that was also run by an Irishman: Seamus. We had a nice bright upstairs room that time. I'm not sure if the reason we had to move on so many times was because we were bad for business. Because the venues were usually quite small function rooms they were more intimate than massive screaming mixed discos that were around the place at the time.

Once when we were at a women's disco upstairs somewhere or another, there were these two women who nobody knew, but they kept on coming up to people on the dance floor and at the bar, everywhere really. I took no notice of them until I lit up a joint. One of them came up to me and asked if she could score some joints of dope off me. I was amused by her lingo, but thought nothing else of it. I'd already brought some dope for a few of me mates at the disco, so I said, 'Yes I'll bring some over for a joint in a bit to ya.'

The next thing I knew was when Robyn, Maddy's girlfriend, came up to me and said, 'D'ya know the women who just came up to you?'

'No,' I said, a bit puzzled. 'She just asked me if I could sell her some dope. Why?'

'Oh fuck, she's only a bleedin' copper. Jan recognizes her,' Robyn said, nodding over at Jan.

'Oh shit, what the fuck am I gonna do now? I thought it was funny how she asked me like she didn't know properly what to say,' I said, panicking a bit. 'I bet she'll think I'm a fuckin' drug dealer now. Great.' I thought of a time a few months ago when two women came to a women's event, left, and then it got raided minutes later for not having a proper license to sell alcohol. Fuck, fuck, fuck was all I could think. How the shittin' hell was I gonna get out of here in one piece? What about Hannah? She wasn't used to this sort of thing. They'll think I'm a proper drug dealer, they'll never believe that I only brought it for my friends. I'll end up in prison. What if they arrest Hannah? They'll raid our house and find dope in her room - we could both end up in prison. Mum's gonna fuckin' kill me. How could I have been so stupid? Panic, panic.

'Listen, I've got an idea,' Robyn said, with a twinkle in her eye. 'They've been up dancing all over each other since they got here, like they're together. So, I'll go and get the girlfriend to dance with me and you go and tell her,' she nodded at the one who'd asked me for the dope, 'that you'll go to the toilets and you'll meet her in there in a few minutes. Meanwhile you and Hannah make a quick exit, and if it is a set up and they're not together, that other woman will get a shock when she has me all over her,' Robyn said, laughing out loud. 'It's cool. They all know what's going on and if the worst comes to the worst they'll all crowd round them so they won't be able to get ya. Ok?' Robyn said, glancing over at Jan and all her other mates.

As I looked over, it seemed like the whole disco knew and were trying to put the plan into action. I had about twenty knowing looks all at once. Hannah had to leave with me because we looked too alike for her to stay.

Robyn puckered her lips to make me laugh. 'Here goes, I'm all yours,' she said. She put her arms out, pretending that she'd already started dancing with the woman, then walked over to her and took her by the hand onto the dance floor and started dancing very close and sexy. Whether the woman was a dyke, before Robyn got her up close and sexy, is another story. She loved Robyn's moves on her. The other woman didn't bat an eyelid at her supposed girlfriend's actions, proving further that it was probably a set up.

I casually walked over to the woman who had asked me to sell her dope. 'D'ya wanna go in the toilets and I'll meet you in a couple of minutes?' I said to her, smiling.

'Yeah, great. See you there,' the silly copper lady said.

She walked off to the toilet. I spun round to see Robyn still engulfing the other one on the dance floor, making sure that she couldn't see me. I walked over to Hannah knowing that she would panic if I told her what was going on. She was stood with Gina and Clare. Gina was always very light and bubbly.

''Ere what you up to, our Cec?' Gina said, laughing.

'Nowt really,' I looked at Hannah.

'What? What ya lookin' like that for?' Hannah said, with fear in her voice and on her face.

'No reason. We've just got to go home, that's all,' I said. 'It's okay - I'll tell you outside.' My face was probably drip white. I was terrified that the place was going to be overrun with police at any second.

'No, tell me now,' Hannah urged me.

'Look, there's two women here who we think are police. One of them's asked me to sell her dope. I didn't know she was a copper and stupidly I said yes. We've got to leave and we've got to leave calmly and we've got to leave now. Right?' I was desperate to get out. Hannah knew that she couldn't stay because of the lookalike thing between us - people did mistake us for each other.

116

'I'll see you outside,' I said, turning slowly to leave.

Hannah walked out after me. I still didn't know what to expect when I got outside. I thought they might be waiting to arrest me but no one was there, thank god. As soon as we got round the corner, we legged it like mad to the tube station and hoped to death that no coppers would come after us!

A few of us went up to Coventry one weekend. We'd made friends with some women up there who used to come down and stay with Erica at Lil's Cafe. On the last night I was there, I met a beautiful black woman in the pub. Diana was her name. We laughed and laughed the whole time we were together. I wasn't sure if she fancied me or not but I knew she liked me 'cos we were getting on so well. I'd like to have said I wasn't bothered if she did fancy me or not, but I fancied her something rotten. She was gorgeous. Beautiful eyes, nose, mouth, skin, everything. All the time we were sitting together in the pub, we hardly said two words to anybody else, just smiling, laughing and chatting to each other. We didn't have any physical contact, apart from sitting very close to each other.

At the end of the night she asked me if I'd like to sleep with her, in a soft and gentle way. I wasn't nervous or shy like I might sometimes be - it felt so natural and flowed with the rest of the night. When we got into bed we sat up and chatted and chatted and chatted and laughed until daylight. We still hadn't even kissed, or anything for that matter! Finally, we laid down and put our arms round each other. It was so peaceful, almost like part of me had come home. She asked me if I minded if we didn't have sex. She said that she didn't want to have sex with yet another white woman. I totally understood what she was on about and felt honored that she could say that to me. We fell asleep wrapped round each other.

The next day we went off to go round to where the others were staying, and as we walked through the streets we held hands the entire way, still laughing and chatting like we had the night before. I've never done that with anybody the next day, never mind someone I've only slept with once.

Punch, Judy & The Crocodile Tears

A load of us from the Stepney squats went away again, only this time it was abroad to Amsterdam. There was a week-long women's music festival on and not only was there our gang of about ten, but we knew of quite a few other women from London who were going as well, mostly performers. We got the ferry across the Channel from Harwich to the Hook of Holland. Going to a country called the same as Hannah's and my surname provided endless entertainment for us. It was like the constant cabaret from our home in Stepney had turned into a travelling circus now that we were on our holidays - yippee!

It was such a thrill to be going abroad as well. We arrived in the day time and struggled a bit to find cheap accommodation as the city was packed with women from all over Europe and America attending the festival. Finally, we managed to get into a hostel called the Hans Brinker. They were full but had an overflow section in an old part of the hostel that used to be a chapel where there were bunks and bedding for all ten of us. It was good because we had the whole place to ourselves, totally separate from the rest of the hostel. Hannah and I didn't really have enough money for the both of us to stay in the hostel, as well as for all the other expenses; as we looked so similar we pretended that we were the same person. I'd stay in bed during breakfast and she would bring my food up from what was put out for us all, which was usually hard-boiled eggs. I made them all laugh when they came back up to the 'chapel' as I would crack the egg open on my head as I sat up in bed to eat it. When we left to go out for the day, I would put on whatever jacket Hannah had worn down for breakfast, just to confuse the people who worked at the hostel into thinking I was her, and when we got outside we would swap them back. There were a couple of spare beds in the 'chapel', so we had a bed each as well.

Amsterdam didn't really seem that exciting on the first day we arrived. I suppose the overnight travelling and no sleep didn't help. But it was a different story after some daytime sleep, and seeing the place lit up in the night-time sky was such a buzz. Not only all the bright neon colors everywhere, but our name was written all over the place as well, Holland this and Holland that. We were all in hysterics. Everything was so different to what I was used to - the trams (that I kept nearly getting run over by), the canals, the houseboats, the bars selling dope, the flowers everywhere, the different people, different language. I absolutely loved it. It felt so much more civilized than anywhere else I'd ever been.

We met Vicky and Alex while we were there (our neighbors from down the road in Stepney). They'd been in the Red Light district where women sit in the window displaying themselves for sex. When one of the women in the window saw Alex, she beckoned her to come in for sex and couldn't quite work out why Alex had refused. It gave everyone a good laugh when she told the story afterwards. There was a bar just for women in Hazenstraat where we spent a lot of our time. It was on two levels - the upstairs bit looked down into the bar area and the surrounding tables and chairs, while there was a wooden stairway in the middle of the room leading up to the main seating area. It had wooden rails all around the edges, so you could look down into the lower bar area if you were sat upstairs. It was all done very tastefully, which made for a great chilled out atmosphere.

Mari, me, Hannah, Gemma and one or two others were sat in the upstairs bit one afternoon when all of a sudden two drunk, rough-looking men walked in. They sauntered up to the bar and ordered drinks. Out of our crowd there was only Mari and me who could see what was going on. The woman behind the bar looked a bit worried but she served them with drinks straight away. I thought, 'Oh shit, there must be trouble if she's served men in a women's bar.' One of the men was in his 30s, tall and fat with a raincoat and hat on. They were both drinking a white spirit, probably the Dutch firewater Jenever. The other man was older and smaller with a dark hat and coat and was wearing glasses. They were laughing and talking so loudly that I knew there was going to be trouble. They'd clearly come in deliberately because they knew men weren't allowed. The next thing I knew, the tall fat man pulled out a gun and waved it around the room, pointing it everywhere, including up into the top bar where we were still all sitting. For a split-second I thought that my life was over, just like that, taken by a pissed up scheisser. He put the gun on the bar, necked his drink, roared with laughter and then he and his scrawny sidekick staggered off out of the bar as he stuffed the gun back into his coat pocket. The rest of our group finally clocked that something had happened, probably when they'd seen the blood drain from mine and Mari's faces and our stunned silence with mouths wide open. Heavy stuff. It was only a couple of months earlier than Hannah and I had seen an undercover policeman get shot dead in the street about a mile up the road from our house. I hadn't properly got over that, never mind this now. I gave the impression that I took it in me stride though, like everything else. It certainly didn't spoil the rest of my holiday.

The main part of the music festival was in a massive center called the Melkveg (the 'Milky Way' in English). It had so many different parts to it all, and felt so relaxed and laid back. Maddy and

Robyn were there with their theatre group. We always had such a laugh with them and their crowd. Another theatre group from London were there too. We knew most of them quite well as Vicky and Alex were part of it. Although I knew every act and song in their show backwards, from hearing them practicing and going to venues where they were on, I still loved to see them perform. Mari and Hannah laughed at me sitting on my own in the front seat of the balcony, laughing and clapping at their show, while they sat at the back just talking to each other and ignoring it all.

'Ya'd think she'd never seen it, wouldn't ya?' I heard Mari say, laughing to Hannah.

Vicky and Alex had an upset in Amsterdam as Vicky had a fancy for another woman in the show. They were going on tour with the show round other European towns and cities after Amsterdam. Over the weeks we kept hearing reports of blazing rows from various European hot spots. Ella, the woman Vicky had the crush on, had a girlfriend back home - a tall, dark, blue-eyed woman called Mia who I fancied. I didn't know her very well, but round the time of her upset over Ella's roving eye, I kept seeing her out on the scene more and more. I liked her, she was soft and gentle. We talked, I listened, we made love. Ella was furious, I could sense it all the way from whatever country she was in at the time.

After their tour had finished things still hadn't settled down with the gruesome threesome. One night we had a party after the pub at our house and as usual, it was packed. I wasn't sleeping with Mia anymore, but we were still friends. Alex was very drunk before she even got to the party and the stupid mind-fuck Vicky invited Ella to our party in hopes of some drama methinks. Alex's drunken state was quelled so far by anger at Ella's presence. As I walked past her in the hall, she looked at her trousers and said, 'There'll be blood on these white trousers tonight and it won't be mine.'

I looked at her and held her menacing drunken glare. I thought, 'Not in this fuckin' house there won't, lady.' I felt sorry for her, being treated so badly by Vicky for so long. It was Ella's blood she wanted, not Vicky's. I knew really that she wouldn't spill blood, but I wasn't taking any chances. I kept my eye on her all night.

Hannah and I both went up to talk to her to see if we could calm her down a bit, just to be friendly really, bringing her into our fold. She didn't like it at first - maybe she could see that we were trying to calm her down.

'You think I wank behind my back,' she said to both of us. I was slightly confused - was she a contortionist? My mind really was going down that path!

'No, we don't,' Hannah said anxiously. We were standing either side of her and looking at her, to genuinely help with her distressed state. Hannah was quite upset by Alex's distress; she didn't like to see anyone in such a bad state. I wasn't that bothered, to tell you the truth. I didn't want to see a fight and I was a bit pissed off that yet again Vicky was getting all this avoidable attention. On top of this, it all made Alex look like the baddie and Vicky look like the victim - the usual twisted way that Vicky operated. Alex tried to make a grab at Ella when she saw her in the hallway but Hannah and I jumped in to stop her. Ella and silly Vicky left after their fucked-up floor show had finished, thank christ. We could get on with our party.

It was a few months after we'd moved down before Hannah managed to get a job. She was able to keep herself occupied alright, considering everything was very new to her and she would be on her own all day, while me and Gemma were at work. We both spent nearly all of our time together. It was funny because before we moved to London we didn't get on very well, we seemed to clash a lot. It was Bernie who helped me more than anyone else, gay or straight, and I think she helped Hannah as well. When it came to me moving down to London, it was Bernie who stepped in and linked us up together. Hannah was talking of coming to London with her straight friend from school, to work in a hotel together. So, Bernie tentatively stepped in between Hannah and I, with each of us sitting on either side of her. She was smiling and wanting to laugh so I knew she was up to something as did Hannah.

'Look, I know you two don't get on and I can see why,' Bernie said, looking at each one of us and laughing. 'But I get on really well with both of you, and you're the only two dykes in the family, so I think you should both move down to London together. You don't want to move down with that straight woman, Hannah, and you'll be lonely without me or Kate there with you,' she said looking at me. We both looked at Bernie, then at each other.

'Okay,' I said, pleased that Bernie had openly acknowledged that we didn't get on and had been strong enough to say so out loud. Hannah agreed to the joint move as well.

We never spoke of our differences. We weren't used to speaking that much to each other because apart from not getting on, we lived in different cities. I was in Lancaster and Hannah was at Mam and Dad's in Manchester. We'd spent a bit of time together, but only because one or other of us was seeing Bernie. All that changed, of course, now we had to make this big decision to move away together. I was pleased that she'd made her own decision (even though Bernie had prompted it). I stopped resenting her for being a dyke and was excited at the thought of all our future adventuring together. I knew I'd have to take her under my wing for a while, that went without saying really. I didn't mind though as I knew we would have a laugh. I'd seen what good times she and Bernie had together.

We got on very well from that day, after Bernie's pep talk. Hannah loved meeting lots of new women in London. Being only eighteen she hadn't been out on the scene as much as I had. When she lived at Mum and Dad's she sneaked off into the Manchester gay life the odd time, and made the odd trip up to the Lancaster women's scene (a lot less conventional than Manchester). Most people we met were thrilled to meet us both, some said we were like a breath of fresh air, always laughing and living life to the full. Vicky and Alex, particularly Vicky, would occasionally make sniping comments that I was Hannah's bodyguard and that no one dared to cross her, for fear of retaliation from me. I just laughed and ignored them. My mother always said to me, 'If anyone tries to put you down, they're usually jealous,' so I never took much notice of their silly sniping. Why anyone would want to cross a young eighteen-year-old woman, who was always warm and friendly to them, I don't know. Both of them were about ten years older than her as well, neither of them worked for a living, and they mostly just hung about all day playing music or drinking wine from a case that Vicky's daddy had dropped off. They always had plenty of money to do whatever they wanted.

Of the two of them, Vicky was the real troublemaker - I think Alex just went along with whatever Vicky was instigating. We'd often hear about some drama or another kicking off in their house, usually involving members of the theatre group that they were in. Vicky was one of those people who wasn't happy unless there was some kind of drama going on around her. I think it annoyed her that Hannah wasn't easy prey, like she'd probably imagined when she first met her. One time, not long after we'd met Vicky and Alex, they were at our house one night, socializing with us two and Gemma. Vicky had rolled a joint and passed it to me. After I smoked some of it I got a terrible burning sensation on my forehead, right where your third eye is supposed to be. I couldn't understand what it was about - I hadn't done anything different at all, just smoked her joint. My forehead wouldn't stop hurting me, and I kept going on and on about the terrible burning pains that I had. Vicky just kept laughing. Eventually it eased up to be just about bearable, at which point Vicky looked at me and Hannah with a really stupid grin on her face.

'What do you think of that joint?' she said, lurching forward.

'Nothing, it's just a joint, why should I think anything of it?' I said, wondering what madness she was up to now.

'Oh, it's because it had heroin in it,' she said, gloating like she'd just done the scam of the century and tricked these naive Northerners into taking heroin. Ha, ha, what a laugh - not. I shrugged it off like it was nothing, so she didn't get a shred of satisfaction from her stupid childish prank. I was amazed though at my forehead, like my third eye was warning me of the spiked joint. I was so taken with this idea that it defused a lot of the anger I would have otherwise had towards fuckwit Vicky.

Another time I was coming home from work, I'd been on an early shift at the hospital and the day before I'd been on a late shift, and didn't get home until gone eleven at night. I hadn't seen Hannah 'cos she was out when I got home the night before and in bed when I had left at 6.30 the following morning. Everything was as it should have been as I walked home from work and down our street – that was until my key wouldn't get in the keyhole for my hands shaking. I was suddenly, totally out of the blue, really, really angry.

I went down to the kitchen in the basement. Hannah was standing at the cooker frying some onions and Gemma was sitting at the table. As soon as I saw Hannah's face I knew that Vicky and Alex had done something awful to her.

'What's happened? What have they done now?' I demanded to know. Before she could answer, Gemma stood up from the table.

'Look Cec, you know what they're like,' she said, half smiling as if it was okay to be like them. She'd always sucked up to them because she thought they were so fuckin' famous, with the band they used to be in and the theatre group now and their money.

'You can shut it an' all,' I said to her, spinning round and pointing my finger. She sat down as quick as she'd stood up, and she did shut up an' all.

'Go on, what've they done?' I asked Hannah again.

She told me that she'd been at their house, playing the guitar and having a jamming session with them - they had all their band instruments set up in their house all the time. Hannah loved to play the guitar. She'd had lessons after school, so was thrilled at them asking her to play with them and other female musicians. She said it was great at first, but as it got later Vicky started to ask her what she thought about abortion. She knew full well that Hannah had had a very strong Catholic upbringing and that Catholics were often very outspoken about the evils of abortion. They also knew how young she was and that it wasn't actually that long since she'd left school, having stayed on to study for more qualifications rather than leave at the first opportunity as so many young women did.

They knew fine well that it was a very controversial issue and that Hannah wouldn't have had time to develop her own opinions on the subject, not enough to stand up to them thugs anyway. There were two other women with them as well. Hannah kept saying to them, 'I don't know what I think properly,' but they kept taunting her with their vicious tongues, like they were back in the dormitories of their boarding schools. When she tried to leave they blocked the door and wouldn't let her get out of the house. That was it - bingo! All the fireworks inside of me, that had made my body shake so much, erupted when I heard that they stopped her leaving the house. She said it was only when she started crying that one of the other women there came to her rescue and insisted that they let her go. I made a start towards the door and Gemma moved towards me in her seat.

'Cec don't do anything stupid,' she said in her prissy voice.

'Fuck off,' I said angrily to her over my shoulder.

I flew up the stairs and took my nurse's uniform off before putting my jeans and shirt on, ready to go out and fuckin' kill the bastards! I knew they'd waited for their chance to intimidate her while I was out of the way on long work shifts. I say 'they', but again it was Vicky who had set it up. I knew that for sure Alex wasn't really like that and was more a mug than anything else. That doesn't excuse her though; she'd taken part in it alright. I got out onto the street into the hot evening sun and marched down to their door. I banged on their door knocker as hard as I could. A small long-haired woman called Mel answered - she played music with them.

'Is Vicky in?' I asked her, my face fuming.

'Look, we don't want trouble, there's already trouble going on here today,' she said a bit desperately, looking back over her shoulder into the hallway.

'Is Vicky in?' I said again loudly, but slower and clenching my teeth. Vicky of course, being a fly round shit when it came to trouble, came running through the hallway and pushed her pale doughy face over Mel's shoulder. Alex, as usual, followed behind her and pushed her face over Mel's other shoulder, like it was a Punch & Judy show. So I put my finger up and pointed sharply at her. 'And you can fuck off an' all.'

One wrong word or move from either of them again, and they would have had a punch on the chin, one fist each at the same time. I could've decked them without a doubt. The anger alone could have knocked them over without me lifting a finger.

'How dare you stop my sister from leaving a room, how dare you speak to her like that, if you so much as breathe near her again, I will kill you both. How dare you!' I roared in the most threatening voice of my entire life. I meant it as well, I felt like I could have killed them with my bare hands.

'I have kept her together and looked after her so well in the months that we've been here, not to have a stupid shit like you spoil it all in one breath. I'm warning you.'

Needless to say when you challenge bullies they back off immediately, being the cowards that they always are underneath. I turned round and walked back down the street to our house and went in the front door, this time firework free.

Hannah and Gemma were still in the kitchen when I got back in. I walked down the rickety wooden steps to the basement and as I got back to the open kitchen door, I held my jaw and started moaning like I'd been punched in a fight. Hannah and Gemma screamed laughing.

'You should see the state of them two,' I said pretending to dust me hands together like I was finishing a big fight. 'They couldn't fight their ways out of a paper bag, pair of drippy kids. They're pathetic,' I said, sitting down. 'Aye well, they picked the wrong ones to start on this time, I can tell ya,' I said, looking up at Hannah. She looked confident again, thank god.

'What happened? What did they say?' Hannah asked me.

'Oh, nowt really. I just said that I was going to kill them,' I said laughing.

'Really?' Hannah said, wide eyed and grinning.

'More or less, yeah,' I paused. 'Well if they ever pull a stunt like that again, I said I would kill them. They knew I meant it an' all.'

Hannah laughed. 'Go on, tell me what happened,' she continued.

There was a knock at the door. All three of us looked up.

'That'll be them, I bet ya,' I said.

'I'll get it,' Gemma said as she stood up. Hannah looked at me.

'You just carry on cooking,' I said, nodding at her. 'You can handle her, Hannah.'

We could hear Gemma letting someone in. 'Is it her?' Hannah said, laughing.

'I think so,' I whispered, grinning and wanting to get hysterical laughing. Gemma came in first and sat down opposite me at the table. Silly Vicky followed after her and just stood at the doorway, staring in at Hannah, who was still cooking.

'Hannah,' Vicky started speaking in a pathetic voice, pretending that she was upset. What a joke.

'Yes, what d'ya want?' Hannah retorted.

'I'm so sorry,' Vicky said still in a pathetic voice. She then started squeezing some water out of her eyes (if I said tears I'd be lying). She carried on just standing there, waiting for Hannah to offer her some forgiveness or something. Just game playing really, mega attention seeking.

'Don't come round 'ere with your crocodile tears,' Hannah said, barely looking up from her cooking. I was thrilled at her words - I'd never heard that expression before. It was ace that she just said it entirely independently from me. So much for them thinking that I pulled her strings. Bastards. Vicky looked like she was stuck to the doorframe, like she had no intentions of leaving until we gave her what she wanted. She just craved attention. She just kept staring in at Hannah, probably too scared to look at me.

'Right, go on now, you can get out. We're 'avin our tea,' I said, waving my thumb up towards the stairs. She had no choice but to slope off out of it, at last. That was it, game over!

Me and Hannah went out to the pub that night as normal. Vicky and Alex were both in. We said hello to them and carried on like they could never touch us, and they never could. We carried on socializing with them again after a while. It would take more than a spoilt brat like Vicky to upset either one of us for any length of time.

The Mad Axe Woman

Jackie, the other woman gardener who worked in the park where I was based, had become my friend although we hardly ever saw each other outside of work hours. We had such a laugh all the time. She was nearly as tall as me with dyed blonde shortish straight hair and blue eyes - a bit boyish some might say. She hadn't worked at the park for very long before I started working there. Born in Bow in East London, she couldn't have been more cockney if she tried. She talked to me a lot about the East End. I was fascinated by some of her stories, such as how she and her mates used to frequent the Blind Beggar pub on the corner of Whitechapel Road, after the Kray Twins shot someone dead there. It became 'the place to go' for a while after that gruesome incident.

The gay scene that Jackie lived in was a totally different one to mine, so much so that that no one in the scene I was in had any idea about it. She told me that she used to go to a club in West London called The Aztec; I didn't like the sound of it at all.

Very occasionally we'd arrange to meet up in a club that we thought both her friends and my friends would like. We meant well but somehow it never once worked out that both parties liked the clubs, never mind each other. Me and Jackie were always pleased to see each other. Some of her mates were rock hard - you didn't dare smile and say hello in case people thought you were after their bird, their cockney sparrow! In some places, from the second I walked in I thought some crackpot butch would try to punch me lights out. To them I must've looked cocky, just walking into a place and never mind averting my eyes, but also smiling at everyone. The vibes were massive from the butches. I always made sure that I looked them in the eye though, especially the most threatening ones, even if it was only for a second. I let them see that they wouldn't win a fight if they took me on and that despite my placid nature, I would kill if I was pushed far enough. Luckily no one ever did try to find out for sure.

I think I was a lifeline for Jackie as her gay scene seemed very constrained to me. There seemed to be lots of deceit and a big pressure to stay in the closet. Although there were people sleeping round in my scene, and sometimes with your girlfriend whether you agreed or not, at least it was more out in the open and other women would be around you if you did reach rock bottom. Nearly everyone was out of the closet in my scene, as hard as it sometimes was, and this gave us some strength as a group. Jackie's scene was mostly working-class women and mine was mostly middle class (or so it seemed). The pressure on the women in Jackie's scene was immense - to have to live a complete lie about your sexuality doesn't bear thinking about. Unsurprisingly, Jackie had been off work sick before she was a gardener, with depression and agoraphobia for quite a while and she still struggled a little bit when I first met her. Jackie loved to hear my tales from the mad goings on in my life - it was like a living lesbian soap opera! She'd never met anybody like me before. I liked to listen to her stories as well, and about how not long ago, the police would raid gay clubs in London and have everyone pinned up against the wall. 'Thank god I missed that era,' I thought when she told me.

I wish I'd also just missed meeting Jackie's girlfriend as one night she turned up at our house and gained the title 'mad axe woman'.

It started out as any other ordinary day at work would. We'd had our early morning breakfast in the greasy cafe next to the park with the blokes from my work gang and Lee the tractor driver, who Jackie sometimes hung around with. Ya could tell it was gonna be a scorcher that day, even at that time of morning it was quite warm. We said goodbye after breakfast. I went off on my own to do some work on one of the estates and Jackie headed to do some tree work. She had a lot of heavy-duty cutting equipment in the boot of her car to do the job.

At about eleven o'clock, as the sun was really starting to warm the place, Jackie turned up out of the blue. It looked like she was up to something. Usually she only worked inside the park and couldn't escape from the bosses in the depot office as I could, working on the outside. Today, because she was doing tree work, she didn't have to plan to escape because she was working on some trees outside of the park. Her girlfriend, like a lot of girlfriends in her scene, was very possessive and kept Jackie on a very tight lead. Both their lives seemed very restrictive to me. I suppose it was no wonder Jackie had bunked off work after only a few hours to come and find me. Any chance for a taste of freedom.

West London was the place at the end of her escape tunnel with lunch in a pub with a woman she fancied from ages ago. Jackie had arranged it all before she had even got to me. So off we went across London in her car. She always looked far too clean and well dressed for work as a gardener, probably because most of her day was spent skiving off. I took my overalls off and just had a t-shirt and some second-hand dress trousers on. I didn't look too dirty to go into a West End pub but I was still wearing my steel capped work boots, so I tried to hide them while we were sat in the pub by putting my feet under the seat whenever any bar staff walked past.

Alice, the woman we were meeting for this secret rendezvous, worked in an office near the pub. She seemed nice and we chatted and laughed for ages. I was pleasantly surprised by how relaxed it all was. Jackie's present girlfriend Ginny was a scary character. Of all the women in the pubs and clubs I had been in with Jackie, Ginny was the most unnerving. She was only small, not capable of much you might think, until you looked into her eyes. Then your mind wouldn't just be changed, but razed to the ground by her steely-blue, psycho eyes.

One drink led to another and there was no mention of anyone going back to work. Alice invited us back to hers after the pub for even more drinks - phew, I was very pissed. When we got back to Alice's flat, I started to show them some yoga moves that I had recently learned and they were in hysterics. Fuck knows how I managed to even stand up, never mind practice yoga.

It wasn't long until the mood changed. Jackie started slagging Alice off each time she left the room, calling her a slut and a tease. It was horrible. Jackie herself went to the toilet at some point and when she came back she started accusing me of getting Alice's phone number, so that I could ring her and arrange to see her behind Jackie's back. It was all very stupid; I wasn't interested in any kind of deception. She wouldn't believe me no matter what I said. Then I noticed Alice's number written on the phone.

'Look, there's her number written on the bloody phone, I could have just gone and got it myself if I wanted it. She didn't have to give it to me,' I said, despairing about this mad mood swing.

'Oh yeah, I suppose that's true,' Jackie said, finally believing me, thank god.

We left Alice's somewhat worse the wear for drink. Somewhere along the line Jackie had phoned her girlfriend Ginny to tell her a cock-and-bull story as to why she wasn't home on time from work. She told her that I'd cut my hand and that she'd had to take me to casualty. We somehow got all the way over from West London to Stepney in one piece. Fuck knows how Jackie managed to drive, the drunken state we were both in. Hannah and Mari were at home when we got back to mine. They'd never met Jackie up close and personal before, having only seen her at a distance in a club with me on the odd occasion. They both thought she was quite fanciable. Instead of Jackie heading off home when we got to ours, she decided that she was in the mood for even more to drink, once she'd seen Mari and Hannah. It seemed like it was more than just drink she fancied! Her day of freedom obviously wasn't anywhere near over, since she hadn't had a kiss or a whisper of anything from Alice. Mari and Hannah were in hysterics at me and Jackie coming in drunk. We must've looked like a double act when they first saw us walking in together. The four of us went round to the B.P for a drink.

After about an hour Mari and Hannah left with Jackie and I following not long after. When we got back in the house Mari said that the next-door neighbors had been round to tell us that the Fire Brigade had been round to our house with blue lights flashing as someone had called them out. I was very puzzled so I went to speak to our Asian neighbors. The man who came to the door told me that after the Fire Brigade came, a woman was knocking on their door and said that she had to get into their back garden, to get into our house because her 'husband' was in there. He let her through to our back garden. I came back and told the others what he'd said. Jackie's face said it all when I told her.

'Quick, run and put a bandage on your hand,' Jackie said to me in a blind panic. 'It's Ginny, she's here.'

I dived downstairs and quickly wrapped a bandage around my hand, then shot back to the hallway upstairs where Jackie and Mari were standing. Hannah came down the stairs from the top half of the house.

'All the windows in your bedroom have been smashed,' Hannah said, looking terrified. Mari put her head into the front room on the ground floor.

'These at the front are smashed as well,' she said.

I could see a small figure through the glass at the back door, just standing there staring in at us.

'Cec, open the door. I want to speak to you,' the spooky figure spoke.

'No, you've smashed all our front windows, how do I know you're not gonna smash the back ones as well?' I shouted through to spooky Ginny.

'I won't. I just want to talk to you,' the ghost said.

'No, go away. If you smash any more windows I'll phone the police. I mean it,' I continued, trying to fend her off.

'Where's Jackie?' the eerie figure said, moving away from the door.

Me, Jackie, Hannah and Mari just stood in the hallway looking at each other, wondering what to do.

'She's gone,' Hannah whispered.

'No she aint. She won't go 'til I come out,' Jackie said, looking freaked out and very pale.

'You can't go out. Fuck knows what she'll do,' I said, looking round the hall to see what we could do to get out of the mess that we were in. Everything was a bit swirly. Me being so drunk was blurring not only my vision, but also the true reality of what was going on - being trapped in our hall by a violent specter-like freak. No one was coming up with an escape plan, then all of a sudden there was a knock at the front door. We all jumped with fear as the noise reverberated down the hallway. Then Ginny's scary voice sounded again, this time through the letterbox.

'Cec, open the door.'

We all looked terrified towards the letter box! Hannah was sat on the stairs a bit of the way up and staring down at the door.

'Fuckin' 'ell. What we gonna do? She's already smashed our windows.' Hannah said, scared shitless. The ghost spoke again, this time her voice a bit quieter and even more eerie.

'Cec, go on, just open the door. I don't want any more trouble.' The ghost was wailing and pleading with me to see sense and put an end to all this madness.

'I could sort this out. All I needed to do was open the door. She can't be all that bad. Listen, her voice is soft and reasonable now. She just wants her girlfriend to go home with her nicely, we never should have gone off to see that other woman in the first place. It'll all come to an end when I open that door,' I insanely and drunkenly thought. I staggered towards the door and pulled back the latch. That was the split second the psycho lunged into the door with the most vicious, most deadly, tree-cutting implement that she could lay her hands on from Jackie's car. I pulled my face back as fast as I could and tried to push the door closed.

By the grace of god, (as my Mum always says), it was also the same split second that Hannah had dived off the stairs and thrown herself at the door, forcing it shut, saving me by a hair's breadth from fuck knows what. I'd have been struck in the face by a viciously sharp blade. Jesus... it doesn't bear thinking about. I probably owed my life to Hannah that day.

Jackie insisted on going outside after a while and leaving with Ginny. She didn't want us to have any more trouble. I said she didn't have to go, but I think she knew that Ginny wouldn't leave until she'd gone. I was worried for her but she wouldn't have it any other way and said she knew how to handle her. I couldn't quite see how myself. Unarmed Jackie, heavily armed psycho specter. I just had to hope that she wouldn't kill her. That's all I could hope for, really.

Jackie phoned me fairly early the next day to say that she'd pay for a glazier to come round. Luckily, it was a Saturday so we were off work. She also said that shed managed to stop Ginny from trying to kill her, not just with a lethal assortment of gardening chainsaws, axes, you name it, but also with a car. Apparently, Ginny kept trying to crash the car with them both in it and then tried to run Jackie over after she'd managed to get out. And all for one day's freedom. Needless to say, I never jumped ship with Jackie again.

You're Upset, I'm Upset,
We're All Upset

The time had finally arrived for me to say farewell to Kate. I could never stop seeing her, no matter what was happening but my feelings towards her had changed tremendously. The desperate heartache, that I'd felt for some of the three years that I'd known her, had all but withered into mildly irritating intolerance on my side of the fence. Kate had enough of London, and of England as well. She'd got a one-way ticket to Greece and found herself some kind of teaching job to go to. She wanted us to go out for a curry at the Nazrul on Brick Lane where a few of us used to go for our tea on a Sunday. I'd asked her the night before if she wanted me to stay over at her new abode in Hackney. I said that I needed to know because if I was, then I would need to bring my work boots for the next day. She didn't like me asking - I think she thought I was being too matter of fact and dismissive of her feelings towards me. Maybe she was a bit deluded about how I might have felt, after the past dreadful year we'd had together in London, since we'd both arrived down here. Either way she eventually decided that she wanted me to stay over.

Being a gardener didn't do a lot for your weekday love life, if you wanted to stay over at your lover's place for the night. Apart from the early start, you had not only your massive steel capped boots, but your overalls and casual clothes and donkey jacket to think about and to organize. I managed to get it down to just the boots on this occasion and had them in a carrier bag on the floor next to me in the Indian restaurant. Not the coolest thing to have with you. Kate didn't seem too bothered as she knew only too well what I was like with not caring about what other people thought.

The evening started off quite stilted really, once I'd finished saying hello to Ali, the Indian chap who owned the Nazrul, or 'The Naz' as we called it. Kate seemed to be living in a different reality to me. She was acting like it was our very first date or something and just completely ignoring the general demise of our relationship. I couldn't cope with this silly flirting and stupid pretense. We'd ordered our food and were sitting waiting for it to arrive. The thought of spending the whole night with her was too daunting for me. She was really doing my head in despite the distinct possibility that this would be the very last time that I'd see her. I asked her if she would mind if we didn't sleep together that night. It was the first time I had ever said that to her.

A fierce, dark cloud descended over the entire restaurant. It was already a hot evening, but now the humid heat could've melted the steel on my capped boots. 'Oh shit,' was all that I could think after seeing the dreadful look on Kate's face.

'Don't you dare say another word to me,' she said, breathing electric lightning over me, before the thunder was about to clap me around the ear hole and the dark cloud burst all over the restaurant.

'I'm going to cause the biggest scene, right here and now, that you will ever know.' Kate sparked out at me, like a lightning conductor with ten thousand volts inside her. I was so embarrassed and absolutely dreading what her next move was going to be. I had a good relationship with all of the people that worked at the restaurant. Ali, the owner, treated me like royalty every time I came in. I'd never be able to show my face in there again. What the fuck was she going to do? I kept my head and braced myself for the storm about to strike and do its worst. I could've done with one of those underground storm shelters like in 'The Wizard of Oz'. The twister approaches and everyone but Dorothy just about manages to open the doors and get in out of the way of any flying objects and doors that might crack you on the head, and send you off to face the wrath of the wicked witch, formerly of Wingate Street!

Oh dear, what would Dorothy do if she were here? Kate didn't say another word, but stood up, grabbed her coat and left. As she stormed out, the waiter walked over to my table with all our food and gently laid it all out in front of me. Dish after dish laid down on the table, with a tropical storm raging all around me. The waiter bowed his head and smiled at me when he had finished putting the last dish on the table. I bowed my head and smiled back at him.

'Thank you,' I said. He smiled and bowed his head one more time, before returning to the counter. 'He's going to think I'm bonkers when I get up to pay in a minute and I haven't touched any of the food,' I thought. I stood up, composed myself and walked up to the counter, where the waiter was stood sorting out the orders.

'My friend had to leave in a hurry, so I have to follow her,' I said, looking at the open door of the restaurant. I waved a £10 note at him.

'How much do I owe you?' I said, smiling and cringing slightly.

'Here, here it is,' he said, picking the bill up. He handed me the bill and I gave him the tenner.

'Thank you,' I said, smiling at him again, 'Sorry about all that, we haven't eaten any of it if you want to give it to someone else.' I shrugged my shoulders and wished that the storm shelter would open its doors and swallow me up.

'It's okay,' the waiter said, putting his hand up and smiling. He gave me my change and I left, not forgetting my steel-capped work boots, of course, that miraculously hadn't dissolved in all the terrible heat of the night.

When I got outside onto the street there was no sight or sound of Kate anywhere, only the buzz of Asian men in their long white robes and caps, returning home after evening prayer. The odd car drove slowly up the street, carefully avoiding the men in white, as they passed chatting to each other from either side of the road. I loved this summer evening scene usually - the heat and the aromatic smell of all the different spices coming from the many Indian restaurants along the lane. More or less everyone in sight was Asian. I always felt like I was on my holidays; the joy of being here in Brick Lane never ceased to please me. But tonight I felt lost. I couldn't see Kate anywhere as she'd disappeared, gone forever it seemed. I just carried on walking down the street, holding my carrier bag with the work boots in it. Each step I took was a reminder that this was it - my marriage finally over.

Bernie, my sister, had moved back from Lancaster to Mam and Dad's in Manchester to do a year-long college course. It was only a couple of weeks until Christmas when I got a phone call from her, to tell me that Dad had thrown Mam out and was being a complete arsehole. Dad was like a lot of men, living the single life within a marriage. He came and went as he pleased, drank and smoked as much as he wanted and chased after other women. He had never been one for holding down a full-time job for any length of time either. Mam had supported him financially as well as looking after all of the children for quite a few years now.

Grace, the youngest, had just left school at sixteen and Miriam still lived at home. She was seventeen and my brother Joe, eighteen, was on a couple of months' leave from the merchant navy at the time of this major upheaval. Bernie said that Mam had come home from working as a teacher (she'd qualified when Grace was only four) and was sat in the armchair. Dad, as usual, had been in the pub at dinner time and just waited, also as usual, for Mam to make him his tea. Only on this day she told him to make his own tea, so he told her to get out if she wasn't going to make it for him. So that was it. She got up from the armchair and walked out. All she had was the clothes that she stood up in. She went to stay with my eldest sister Marian who lived a few miles away with her Italian husband and five children.

Dad decided it was his god given right to throw the rest of them out of 'his house', the house that he hadn't paid a penny towards rent or bills for. The four of them had nowhere to go to, so naturally refused and stood up to the old bastard. As Bernie was the eldest she became the spokesperson for the four of them. He spent the rest of his time (in-between going to the pub that is, of course) roaring and bawling at everyone. 'What about me?' was his catchphrase at the best of times, never mind a time like this. Despite Hannah and I living much further away from Mam and Dad than my older sisters, two hundred miles to be exact, we went straight up on the Friday after Bernie had phoned.

Sometimes the older ones in the family seemed in a slightly different world to the younger ones. They didn't seem bothered about their poor mother's dilemma, or the whole sorry mess of it all. We'd always been a bit like two families in one for as far back as I can remember - the big ones and the little ones. It stemmed from meal times, because there wasn't enough room for us all to sit round the table to eat together. We had to have two sittings - little ones first, then the big ones. This division stuck. I couldn't understand their lack of concern for the whole family's mother. I was surprised and puzzled by them.

I finished at half-past one on a Friday and Hannah finished at half-past three every day of the week, so we were able to get a coach at 5pm from Victoria Coach Station. Mam lent Joe her car to pick us up when we got into Manchester and take us the ten miles back to the house where Mam didn't live anymore. We made it just in time for last orders which was at 11pm. Dad was in the pub, of course, and was thrilled to see us. He bought us two pints each seeing as we'd only just got there. Bernie, Joe, Miriam and Grace were sitting a bit away from him, but still at the same table. They were so thrilled to see us and you could see the tension drop in their faces when they saw me and Hannah.

Dad was one side of us with his fellow Irish drinking mate, with Bernie, Miriam, Grace and Joe on the other. It was such a relief to see them, not Dad so much though. I couldn't help but be a bit pleased to see him. Despite him being an old bastard, I still loved him. Within a matter of minutes, he was pouring his heart out to me and crying his eyes out. He was such a stupid fool. I could have killed him for throwing Mam out, just for his own sake, never mind the terrible consequences for Mam. I knew it was too late and that she'd never come back now. This was the last straw in all the madness.

'Why did you throw her out?' I asked him, looking straight into his blue tear-stained eyes.

'I didn't throw her out, she just left,' he roared at me through his wild sandy hair and beard.

'She didn't leave you, you threw her out Dad, you did. She told me herself on the phone. She wouldn't make your tea, so you threw her out.' I spoke very clearly and steadily.

'Thousands of men throw their wives out every day, it doesn't mean that they want them to go,' he spluttered his words out. I shrugged and sighed. There was a silence between us.

'And why d'ya keep trying to throw these lot out as well?' I said to him, nodding my head over in the direction of the others. They all looked over at us when they heard me mention them.

'What?' Dad said, looking at them with a mad look in his eyes, probably the first time he'd looked at them since Mam had left. 'I've never said they had to leave, never,' he protested, looking absolutely bonkers, like he was a wild animal that had been cornered.

'What's the matter with ya Dad? Don't ya think it's absolutely awful for them having their mother thrown out without you now trying to throw them out?' I paused, 'Eh?' I stared at him. He started to cry again. Course he set me off cryin' an' all. He looked up and over at the near-evictees and they all looked at him.

'I'm sorry, I'm sorry, I didn't mean for you all to go' he said, crying. 'Bernie, I'm so sorry,' he said, looking over at Bernie. She moved over towards him and put her arms around his neck - she was crying as well.

'Dad, it's alright, you're just a bit bonkers sometimes. You can't throw us all out. We love you Dad. You've got to stop being mental though, you can't carry on like this anymore. Look how horrible you've been to all of us,' Bernie said, looking round at Grace, Miriam and Joe.

'I know I have, haven't I?" he paused, 'You see, Mammy's left me, that's the problem,' he said, crying again. 'What am I going to do?'

This time he cried out loud. His friend, who had moved away from us earlier, looked over when he heard Dad's wailing. Dad saw him looking at him.

'Brendan, my wife's left me,' he said to his friend, with tears rolling down his face.

'I know, you've told me Des,' his friend said, looking very uncomfortable and sympathetic in almost the same moment.

Dad got his big, dirty-looking, white hanky out of his pocket, took his glasses off and wiped the tears from his eyes. After blowing his nose really hard and putting his glasses back on, he started to compose himself by puffing his cheeks up and blowing big gasps of air out of his mouth. Bernie held his hand on one side of him and I held it on the other side.

'It's a funny world,' he said, looking like a lion that had been tamed with a tranquilizer dart, judging by the pissed-up look in his red eyes. 'It is a funny world, alright,' I said with a sad smile. 'You don't make it any easier though when you keep trying to chuck these out, do you Dad?' I said, glancing briefly at the others, then straight back at him. 'Hmm?' I said, smiling, trying to keep the peace and his attention.

'No, you're right Cec, I don't,' he replied back to me.

'Why don't you just try to stop yourself once and for all?' I said, shaking my head slightly and pausing. 'Just think about it and tell yourself you're not going to do it anymore as you've really upset them. Promise yourself you'll stop it, eh Dad?' I carried on.

'I will, I will, I'm so sorry,' he said, waving his arm up and looking at the others.

We drank up and bought a load of carry-outs to take back to what had recently become a madhouse. Suddenly everyone was happy again. We linked arms with the 'ole fool, one either side of him, as we walked back through the estate laughing and chatting. Unlike all the other fathers, and especially fathers who were now grandfathers, our Dad smoked dope with us when we skinned up after the pub. The odd time he even had his own. I preferred him being stoned rather than pissed out of his head, to tell you the truth. He was far mellower and his sense of humor was a lot more astute. I could talk to him a lot easier as well and I even believed him when he said he wouldn't try to throw them all out again.

Joe took me, Bernie, Hannah, Miriam and Grace up to see Mam the next day, all six of us squashed in the tiny little car together. We all had our tea at Mam's new temporary home, Marian's house, and stayed until her bed time of 10:30 before Mam took us back home. It was even more of a squash on the way back because Mum had to get in as well. She dropped us at the top of the street so she didn't have to see Dad or the house. We waved Mam off, then went to meet matey-boy Dad in the pub for last orders. Dad was upset that we'd all spent so much time with Mam, but he desperately tried to hide it, seeing as he was making an effort to behave himself for once in his life.

The next day, after another late night of too much booze and dope, we met up with Mam at the top of the street, away from the pub so that Dad couldn't see us. It was all very awkward to arrange, but we managed somehow and went out for Sunday lunch, then a nice walk. On the surface, Mam looked like she was keeping it together but I knew that she wasn't really. I was thrown by this huge split between her and Dad. She'd kept this side of things from us as children. I'd hardly ever seen her and Dad argue, just him shouting sometimes. She'd always managed to present a strong, gentle image to the world, like nothing could ever touch or hurt her, or any of her children. Her love and loyalty for us was fierce, and now here she was, vulnerable and crying because of that tosspot. I couldn't bear to see her so upset - it broke my heart.

It was only Wednesday that Bernie phoned to tell me that Dad had tried to throw them all out again. Shallow promises broken after only a few days. I might as well have asked the barman in the pub that night to make the promise instead of Dad, for all the good it did. I was really mad when Bernie told me what he'd done.

'Right, that's it. The bastard. Wait 'til I speak to him. He promised me,' I ranted down the phone to Bernie. She'd had to wait until he'd fallen asleep in the chair before she could use the phone, because everything was 'his'. His phone, his house, his money, his wife. No mention of his responsibilities at all, or his bad behavior. It was always someone else's fault where Dad was concerned.

I waited until I knew when he'd be awake before I phoned. There weren't many of Dad's children that ever challenged him about even the slightest thing, but Bernie and I would. She was very upset by his latest outburst. I didn't know if she or the others could take much more of his roaring, shouting and general bad behavior. As usual, when he answered the phone to me, you'd never have guessed he was causing so much trouble. His tone was calm and friendly to me…for all of about ten seconds until I started to ask him what was going on and what did he think he was doing throwing them all out again.

'I never said anybody had to leave this house!' he roared like a maniac into my ear, via the phone.

'You did. I have had Bernie on the phone to me earlier really upset. You promised me that you wouldn't upset her again, Dad. Why did you say it if you didn't mean it, eh?' I was roaring nearly as loud as he was, now. There was something about him that could light the blue touch paper in my temperament like nobody else could. Whether it was a deep similarity in us both or what, I don't know, but none the less it felt very powerful to me.

'She's upset, I'm upset, we're all upset.' He continued with his crazy fucked up logic.

'Dad, you have to stop it,' I said, pausing, 'It's only fuckin' Wednesday, I've hardly been home five minutes and you've started again after such a short time,' I said, starting to lower my voice. 'What's the matter with you Dad?' I said softly. He started to cry.

Mammy's left me, Cecily. Bridie's fuckin' gone, what am I going to do?' he carried on crying.

I tried to speak rationally to him: 'Talk to the others, Dad, talk nicely. You've always got on well together, don't fuck it up with them as well as with Mam.'

The mention of Mam's name made him burst into tears again.

'They'll help you with Mam, they'll listen and they'll talk to you both. Just stop trying to throw them out. Look, I'm telling you Dad, you've got to stop it. It's got to stop here and now,' I said with a great urgency in my voice.

'Yeah, you're right, you're right Cec. I'll go and speak to Bernie now. I'll apologize,' he said.

'Good. Good on you Dad. You can do it.' I paused. 'Listen, you phone me tomorrow and let me know how you get on talking with Bernie and the others. In fact, you can phone me anytime you want, you know, night or day. I mean it. We all have to look after each other. I know it's really hard on you at the moment, but they're suffering as well, you know. Their Mam's left, they're bound to be upset, aren't they?' I said, trying to appeal to his better nature.

'Yeah, you're right. I'll go and talk to Bernie now. She's in watching telly.' He paused. 'Thanks Cec, thanks.'

'I love you and so does Bernie and the others, eh?' I said softly.

'Yeah, I know you do,' he said, 'And I love you,' he added, crying softly.

'You take it steady and I'll speak to you tomorrow, alright?' I said.

'Yeah thanks, thanks Cec. Bye now, bye,' Dad said finally.

'See you Dad, see ya,' I said before I put the phone down.

PHEW!! He was hard fuckin' work.

'She's upset, I'm upset, we're all upset. Fuckin' 'ell, what a nutter. It's all about him, all the bleedin' time,' I said aloud to myself and shaking my head, then sighing. 'He's bloody crackers,' I mumbled as I stood up to go and tell Hannah, who was in her room, all about our mad phone conversation.

Dad kept his bonkers behavior up for months so of course no one wanted to live with him. As soon as Mam was sorted enough to rent her own place, Bernie and Grace moved in with her and Joe stayed with them when he was on leave from the navy.

Although Mam was my main concern, I still had to keep an eye on 'himself' (Dad), who was becoming more and more like a tramp as each day passed. One time, I went to see him and we were sitting in the living room after tea. He lit a cigarette up and kept flicking the ash into the carpet. I got up and brought in an ashtray from the kitchen and put it on the arm of his chair for him. Any normal person would be pleased and say thank you for being so kind and thoughtful, but no, not him, Mr Madman.

He roared and roared at me. 'If I want to flick my ash onto my carpet in my own home, without some bloody woman coming trying to clean the fuckin' place all the time, then I will,' he shouted up at the ceiling. I jumped up out of my chair as quick as lightning.

'I tell you what Dad, you live in a shitehole. If that's what you want go on, get on with it,' I said, raising my voice and glaring at him before I headed for the door to leave.

'I'm sorry, I didn't mean you Cec. It's just that Marian came here the other day and started hoovering without even asking me. Don't you go 'an all. I'm sorry for shouting at you,' he said, lowering his voice and looking down at the floor.

I smiled slightly at him. He looked up at me like he was about to burst into tears. I sat on the arm of his chair and put my arm round his shoulder. He smelt stale and musty, more so than the rest of the house. I hated the filthy state of the place, even the carpet was starting to get sticky. I held his massive head in my arms.

'Come 'ere Dad,' I said as I started to cry softly. His hair was on my face, it was sticky and smelt moldy. He started to cry.

'I can't cope anymore Cec, I just want Mammy to come back home.' He paused and then said, 'They've all left me now. All gone to live together and left me on my own.' He bawled and bawled. I stopped crying and threw my eyes up to the ceiling in desperation.

Another time, I was round at his house, we'd had fish and chips and he just scrunched the newspaper wrapper up and threw it onto the floor. We went out to the pub later and he never bothered to pick it up before we left. I wasn't going to risk picking it up, not after the ashtray incident. The newspaper was much bigger than the ashtray - god knows what he would've done if I had picked it up – that could have been a major crime!

Flights & Fancy

I loved going up to see Mam, Joe and the girls, as much as I could throughout those difficult times. We always managed to have a good laugh – and quite often a cry too. I suppose that I got to know Mam a bit better, once she finally had her own place. More often than not I'd hitchhike up to Manchester on my own to see them. Hannah hated hitching. One such time I'd taken a few days off work and hitched north on a Friday afternoon. When I got to the beginning of the M1 motorway slip road, I noticed another woman standing on her own, hitching. She had a sign in her hand saying 'Liverpool'. I had seen this woman the previous week at a rounders game on Highbury Fields. I'd noticed her fixed gaze on me while we were waiting to bat and now there she was again - quite tall, wild dark hair and deep blue eyes... hmm, I could shag her. As soon as she saw me her whole being lit up. I had to walk up to her to get in the queue of other hitchhikers.

'Hiya,' she said, smiling, eyes sparkling.

'Hiya,' I replied, about to carry up on past her.

'I saw you at the rounders game on Sunday, didn't I?' she said in her Liverpool accent.

'Yeah ya did,' I said back to her.

163

'Where ya goin'?' she asked.

'Manchester,' I said.

'Oh right,' she paused, 'Ya don't fancy sharing a lift up to the M62 do you?' she asked me.

'Yeah could do.' I paused. 'It'd be easier with two of us,' I said casually.

'Yeah it would, stand here if you want,' she said, moving her bag. I put my bag down next to hers and looked down at the oncoming traffic.

'Have you been waiting long?' I asked her.

'No, I only got here about ten minutes ago, she replied. 'I'm Mel by the way,' she said, smiling and flashing her sparkling blue eyes at me again.

'Oh, hiya,' I said, pausing. 'I'm Cec. Short for Cecily.' I smiled.

'Hiya Cec, or Cecily,' she said, grinning. I laughed.

We got a lift as far as the service station at Knutsford, about twenty miles south of the M62 motorway. We never stopped talking the whole of the journey, like we had to make the most of our short time together. I knew she fancied me the first time she'd seen me at rounders, but now I felt that she didn't want me to go. She wanted me more and more as we edged up the M1 and then onto the M6. This last lift now would see us go our separate ways. It was getting quite late in the evening and I'd loved chatting to her all this time. I felt that I hardly met any working-class dykes. Well, certainly not Northerners so much these days. It was a breath of fresh air to hear someone with like-minded views to me. To fancy her on top of that was an added bonus!

'Is your Mam expecting you tonight?' Mel asked me after we had been dropped off.

'Yeah she is. She knows what it's like timewise when you're hitchhiking though,' I answered.

'Does she,' Mel paused. There was an electric silence between us. 'It's getting late, isn't it,' she said, then silence again.

'Mmm, yeah it is,' I said.

The electric silence was sparking me up deep inside, all my juices joined up together and swirled around like a river, desperate to burst its banks. 'It'll probably be dark fairly soon, d'ya think?' I said, looking up at the sky.

'Yeah it will,' Mel said, her eyes lighting up again. She put her head down and started to look a bit shy. 'D'ya want to come to Liverpool with me and go over to Manchester tomorrow?' Mel said, raising her head and throwing a bit of sparkle dust at me with her eyes. She paused. 'I'm meeting up with some mates and we're going round the clubs. It'll be a good laugh. Why don't ya come?' she persisted.

'Yeah, I'd like that,' I said, nodding over at a couple of phone boxes nearby.

'Yeah, yeah great. I'll wait 'ere and mind your bag if you want to go and phone your mam,' she said, smiling wide and softly.

'Ok,' I said, looking into her sparkling blue eyes.

I walked over to the phone boxes and dialed Mam's number.

'Hiya Mam, it's me, Cec.'

'Oh, hiya lamb, where are you?" she replied.

'I'm at Knutsford service station further south than Manchester,' I said, made up to hear her voice.

'Oh great, you shouldn't be too long then,' she said, pleased to hear my voice too.

'Well the only thing is it's nearly getting dark you see, and I've met this other woman who's hitchhiking to Liverpool.'

'Have ya? That's great,' Mam said.

'Yeah, so she said I can hitch with her to Liverpool tonight and come over to you in the mornin' when it's light. It's not too far, so it won't take that long to get over,' I said.

'Yeah great, whatever you think is best. I don't like the idea of you hitchhiking in the dark on your own,' Mam said.

'I know. I'll be alright now, as long as we get a lift,' I said, looking through the glass of the phone box to where Mel was standing at the edge of the grass verge that led up to the motorway. She saw me looking over as I was talking and smiled back at me.

'Oh, I'm sure you will get a lift if there's two of you,' Mam continued. She was always thrilled by

166

my visits and I think she quite liked my sense of adventure.

'Yeah I'm sure we will.' My money was running out: 'Oh, listen, there's the pips. I'll ring you tomorrow Mam before I set off.'

'Ok lamb, bye now, bye.' Mam's voice disappeared as the dialing tone took over our connection. I put the phone down and walked over to where Mel was standing, to take up the connection with her. She looked up at me.

'Is she alright with you not going home tonight?' she asked me.

'Yep, she's fine. She's glad I've got someone to hitch with.' I looked deep into her eyes, knowing that we were now free to have wild unadulterated sex - woooww!!! I couldn't wait...

It wasn't long before we got a lift straight into the heart of Liverpool. I was thrilled to be there. I loved the accent, the people, the working-class culture, the liveliness, everything about it. I'd been over a few times when I was a kid as Manchester wasn't a million miles away. Mam and Dad had friends from Liverpool and we saw quite a bit of them. I always wished that we lived in Liverpool and not boring, concrete jungle, council estate Manchester. I was truly made up to be in this vibrant city, especially with a beautiful woman on my arm and one who knew all the gay places to go. What more could I have asked for?

Mel had arranged to meet some of her mates in one of the gay clubs. It was a mixed club and very busy and lively. Her friends, mostly men, were really pleased to see her. They all seemed very nice and were friendly and chatty to me. We danced and laughed the night away, going from club to club until finally landing in her bed at six in the morning. We hadn't actually kissed or touched each other really, the whole time we'd been together. I was desperate to at last have the chance to even kiss her, never mind anything else. To my deep disappointment, she was too pissed and couldn't get herself out of her drunken state to have sex with me. We still had a crackin' night out despite me never getting to shag her. By the time we woke up the next morning it was too late to have sex as I had to make tracks to go to Mam's. We said goodbye and knew we'd bump into each other again in London, as she was a frequent visitor to the big city. I think she was a bit sad at our non-consummation, but we hugged and kissed before I left and got the buzz back straight away from the night before. I'd loved meeting her.

Although I'd slept with lots of different women since I'd lived in London, only Kate has ever been my real girlfriend and that was always on her say-so. If I got close to anyone, it never got anywhere when she was around. So really, as hard as it might seem for even me, Kate was the person I'd been closest to in my entire life. Not long after she left I started seeing Bette, a tall, very good-looking woman who lived in Newcastle-Upon-Tyne. At twenty-nine, she was considered to be an older woman to my twenty-three years. Bette had been heterosexual up until a couple of years before when she'd had her first lesbian relationship. She'd fallen deeply in love with a woman called Miranda. They moved in together and were blissfully happy, that is, until Miranda hit on Bette's best friend and started shaggin' her. I already knew Miranda from when she used to visit Lancaster. She was friends with Gemma and used to come and stay down in London sometimes. She gave the impression that she was somehow better than everybody else - too cool to give a fuck about anyone. She appeared nice to a degree on the surface, but that's all it was. All surface and no depth as far as I could see. She couldn't bear it that I was seeing someone who used to be hers.

Bette had come down to London for a two-week break, to get away from Miranda and the other woman, when we first started our romance. I'd met her once or twice before with Miranda and thought not only was she a very attractive woman, but also had a real warmth about her. I never allowed myself to fancy women who were obviously taken. If I ever found myself getting close to an attractive woman who was already involved I'd always keep one eye on myself. I liked to be respectful. When Bette had come to stay at our house for her break it nearly killed me at first, her being in our house in such a small intimate space. She spent all her time going out with me and Hannah every night, like we always did. She'd be there in the early mornings all sleepy and tousled, still in her nightwear, when I'd be back home skiving off work in my overalls, just me and her in the house. She had Gemma's bed while she was on work sleepovers. We used to sit at the kitchen table drinking tea and eating breakfast for hours. We both really liked talking to each other. We discussed class a lot of the time. I don't think she ever thought about it that much. Although she was from the North East, she was middle class, but spent most of her time with working class people. Class differences had become important to me since I'd moved to London. She liked my passion and my insight.

It was almost a week before we finally burst open the wild pent-up passion that we had for each other. Hannah had gone up north to see Mam and the girls for the weekend, so it was just me and her at night-time as well as some of the days. Gemma came out with us as well, one of the nights, but was off talking to everyone else that night so I had her all to myself. Again, although I'd slept with lots of women, I still absolutely hated making the first move and wanted to run a mile when it was just me and her in Hannah's room (which was Bette's room while Hannah was away) at the end of the night. We'd been sitting up on the bed chatting, laughing and smoking a joint. I loved being with her, but when it came time for us to part, I was terribly nervous. I suddenly went a bit cool and started making moves to go down to my own room. She looked into my eyes with her beautiful, brown eyes.

'Why don't you stay in here with me?' she said, moving nearer towards me. I smiled and looked deep into her heart.

'Okay,' I answered softly. She smiled, moved her body into mine, put her arms around my neck and kissed me softly. I loved this tender passion so much...

We spent the rest of her time in London making love, apart from the odd time that I had to do a bit of gardening, in between clocking on and off at the work's depot. She went back to Newcastle, then came back again for a week. Newcastle didn't suit her much these days. Miranda was doing her head in all the time she was there, even though they didn't live together anymore. It was only a few months before she moved down to London for good; she was here half the time as it was. I was delighted when she moved down. Her house was in Villa Road, Brixton. It was a huge squat and it was in much better nick than our house. Sadly though, it wasn't long before things started to go wrong between us. In fact, just before she moved down, she slipped a disc after lifting me up. She was trying to show me how to lift properly without doing your back in, when all of a sudden her back gave way the second she picked me up. I had to look after her for two weeks while she was laid out flat.

Bette wasn't ready for a relationship with me, or anyone else for that matter. She'd never been able to go out and explore the scene that much, not as a single woman, although I don't know if she was too bothered about that. She'd met a lot of women on the dyke scene in Newcastle and since she met me she'd met loads more in London. We always had an ace time wherever we went, but she had this slight unrest within herself, that as time went by kept popping up nearer and nearer to the surface. She became more distant. Sadly, to make matters worse for both of us, I had fallen in love with her a bit.

After about a year of seeing each other, we decided to go on a make-or-break holiday to Corfu for three weeks, with an Australian couple, Milly and Angela, who I was friends with. We got a flight-only deal and found accommodation when we got there. I was absolutely shitting meself 'cos the only time I'd flown was when I was a kid of eight years, and that was just to Southport. Dad took me, our Joe and Bernie up on a pleasure flight (or should I say fright) round the coast for about fifteen minutes, but it seemed more like fifteen years. Dad did a deal with the man running the trip

- all of us for ten shillings. The man was really fat, with greased black hair and a dark suit. I thought he was overloading the plane, what with Dad trying to get us all in on the cheap. Worse still, I thought the plane would fall out of the sky because the fat man would be too heavy with all of us in as well.

I hadn't realized how scared I was of flying until we decided to go on holiday. I had to have about two pints of lager at ten in the morning to knock me out for the flight. Yuck! The runway in Corfu seemed tiny to me - all I could see was sea and just a little bit of land. I thought my last day was here as we were about to touch down. Corfu was beautiful. I loved it but Bette did my head in. We should never have gone away together. By the time three weeks was up I was ready to get home, even though I had to fly again. But when we got to the airport we discovered we were double-booked on the fight, so we had to go to a hotel until we could get on another plane. Unfortunately when we got to the airport the second time, we weren't booked in on that flight either, or the third flight. This went on for three whole days and I was nearly going out of my mind. Before each flight I had to psych myself up in order to fly, only to be told that we couldn't leave. It was like a cruel, sick joke. I felt trapped on this tiny island with Bette, who was little support to me. We kept being sent to different hotels and one time our taxi didn't turn up so we missed a flight. Another time a mini bus turned up, then broke down outside our hotel and all four of us had to push it down the hill. It was like a comedy horror show. I couldn't sleep all the time it was going on.

By the time the third day arrived, my nerves were totally shattered. We were told to go to the airport again, only to be told we couldn't get on a flight. Even worse, we had to stand next to all the people queuing up to get onto a flight that was going to where we wanted to go. When we started complaining yet again to the holiday reps, they tried to shuffle us out of the way, so all the queuing passengers couldn't hear our terrible plight. That was it, I'd had enough and started shouting at them really loud, so that not only the queuing passengers could hear me, but also everyone else in the vicinity.

'I'm not leaving this airport until I speak to someone from the British Consul. Three days we've been stuck here because you overbooked us on a flight that we've paid for and you still won't give us a flight home. Now I'm telling you - you get us a flight out of here and you get it today, because we are not leaving here!' I pointed my finger firmly at the spot on the ground right in front of me.

'Until you do,' Bette whispered to me. I glared at her. Milly and Angela told her to be quiet, or we'd never bloody get out of here. We then got booked onto a flight to Athens, then supposedly booked onto a flight to Gatwick from there.

It was dark when we finally got on a plane to Athens. Although I was desperately relieved to get onto a plane at last, I was still absolutely terrified – more so than on the flight over, because my nerves were so shot from this huge airport cock-up. Milly, Angela and even Bette were worried about me being on the plane. They suggested that I have a window seat so that I could see out and watch the lights as we left Corfu and then arrived at Athens. All the way there they kept asking me,

'What can you see now Cec?'

'A mountain with a house on it and a light in the house,' I replied, every time they asked. Not realizing, until we almost landed, that the mountain was the wing of the plane and the house with lights was the light at the tip of the wing! It gave us all a much-needed laugh when we worked it out, and thankfully it gave me something to look at all the time we were up in the air.

Of course there was no one to meet us at the other end in Athens as promised. Milly and Angela had to kick off as well this time, before we could get anywhere. I was starting to freak out now. They said we had to sleep on the floor of the airport because there were no flights until the early morning. I couldn't sleep in a bed for the past two nights, so there was no way that I could sleep on a fuckin' floor. I just sat with my head in my hands.

Milly and Angela sat either side of me, putting their arms around my shoulders on and off through the night. Bette slept on the floor along with lots of other people waiting for flights. All four of us were supposedly booked onto a flight that left for Gatwick at 6am but by 5:45 we weren't even anywhere near passport control, never mind a plane. It was the ultimate farce. Milly and Angela were shouting at every person they possibly could to get us on the plane home. I was so past it now, I just wanted to die or be sectioned into the local mental hospital, so that at least my madness could be at home, even if nothing else could.

A small dark-haired Greek woman who worked for one of the airlines came running up to us waving a ticket.

'Ella, Ella, I have a ticket, but there is only one seat on the plane.' She looked at each one of us to see who would have it. Milly, Angela and Bette all looked at me.

'You have it Cec, you have to have it,' Angela said urgently to me.

'Yes,' Milly and Bette said in agreement.

'Come on, you have to go now. Run, run!' the Greek woman said, thrusting the ticket at me and trying to push me forward. All four of us legged it full pelt towards departures - those three were all putting their arms around me as we were running - and telling me that I'd be fine once I was on the plane and not to worry, all the way to passport control.

I kept up the fast pace and only just made it by the skin of me teeth onto the plane. My seat was at the front of the plane and there was an off-duty air hostess sitting along the aisle from me. She was an older woman and had a kindly, pleasant face. She smiled at me and made a friendly comment about me only just getting on the plane in time for take-off. I smiled back and then blabbed on to her about my terrible ordeal and told her that on top of everything I was really scared of flying. She looked a bit cautiously at me and then we both sat back for take-off.

When the plane went up into the sky I was mesmerized by the early morning orange light. It felt like I was moving through a huge real-life picture. It blew my mind. I'd never ever experienced anything like this in my entire life. If I hadn't been so traumatized I would have been in total heaven. It was a great distraction for me. I could see the off-duty air hostess keeping an eye on me all through take-off and after, it made me feel a bit better knowing that someone was looking after me. She walked past me once the seat belt sign was off and turned round to look at me close up. She beamed and said, 'Okay?' I smiled and nodded. I was still only just okay and did manage to stay on the plane for the next few hours without totally flipping out.

The evening I got back I had to get to a gig. Hannah and Mari were in a fairly-newly-formed women's band that I was managing. They were due to play a big gig that night at the Drill Hall which was just off Tottenham Court Road. Then, even worse, two days after that we were all going on a tour of Holland with the band for a week, and flying in another fuckin' plane! I really couldn't think about all that. I'd managed to phone Hannah to tell her I was stuck in Corfu. She was very worried as each day passed and I still wasn't back home.

When the plane landed, I was the first off. I'd taken my bags on as hand luggage, so was able to just speed through and was back home in Stepney fairly quickly. It was Saturday morning at about eleven o'clock. Hannah and Mari had not long been up and were in the kitchen. As soon as I saw Hannah, I burst into tears and flung me arms around her.

'Thank God you're home,' Mari said. 'Hannah's been worried sick about ya. I told her you'd be alright, but she's not been able to settle since you phoned to say you couldn't get on the plane.'

'I know, it's been really awful,' I said, still a bit weepy. All three of us stayed chatting for hours and hours. Despite my appalling lack of sleep and traumatized state, I still wanted to go to their gig that night. I went for a sleep at about three o'clock and Hannah said she'd phone to wake me up at about seven. I didn't hear the phone ring and slept through until about nine the next morning.

Mari and Hannah were worried that I'd be too freaked out to fly to Holland on Monday, but I said that flying to Holland would be nothing compared to what I had just been through. So off we went to Holland on Monday morning. I'd got a sick note from one of me mates who was a nurse and signed myself off work for six weeks. I needed another holiday after Corfu and everything for Holland was being paid for because it was with the band. Just what the doctor ordered - except it wasn't the doctor, it was me. And why not? I'd worked hard all my life. I deserved a decent break for once.

What a laugh we had travelling over to Holland. There was me, Hannah the lead guitarist and singer, Mari the bass player, Amy the keyboard player and singer, and Mia the drummer. Although Amy could be a bit of a drip and even a prat at times, she joined in mostly with the rest of us and we had a brilliant time. Because all the events the band played at were women only, we did get a few women flocking around us. As far as I was concerned, my relationship with Bette was over. She'd slept with someone else about six months ago, to my dismay, so I had even fewer qualms about looking for lust. Besides, it was a golden opportunity with so many different women everywhere we went.

One of the places we went was Utrecht. There was a woman called Eva who was an organizer at the event. She was pretty with dark hair, pale skin and blue eyes and we got on very well. As usual, I was too shy to make a move in Utrecht but she decided to come to the next gig with us, which was in Groningen in the north of Holland. We chatted and laughed together nearly all the way there on the train. The only place we could sleep was with the band; all six of us in one dorm-type room. Me and her stayed out for a while longer, after they'd finished gigging, clubbing and partying, that is. We ended up walking into a little park in the town center just as dawn was breaking and as usual, we hadn't kissed or anything all the time we'd spent together. I loved being with her though - she was soft and so, so sexy.

It was barely light when I sat on a bench beneath a tree. Eva sat on my knee and put her around me and kissed me so softly. We looked into each other's eyes in the magic of the morning's light and slowly made love on the bench, under the sprawling tree. Sexy, sexy woman was she...

Zip Wiring Away

I didn't see Bette at all for weeks. People were quick to tell me that she missed me and asked why didn't I keep in touch with her - a load of liberal claptrap is what I thought of that idea. She injured her back again, then she got her head shaved. I saw her out somewhere and hated how she looked: in my eyes there are very few people who can carry off sporting a shaved head. Bette looked even more troubled with no hair to soften her anxious face. She asked me if I would meet up with her. I felt sorry for her, and concerned about her mental state, so I agreed. She met me from work and was dressed in weird hippie clothes, then she started to pick daisies as we were walking through the park. I was embarrassed enough as it was, when one of the gardeners walked past us earlier and saw her shaved head and mad clothes. Now here she was like a fuckin' kid, picking daisies and expecting me to wait for her. I tell ya, it was the beginning of a bit of a downward spiral for her.

The band had a gig in West London - it was the night-time social at a lesbian conference. Everything was going well, until someone said that there was a group of fascists (namely the National Front) outside the door trying to get in. I shot over to the entrance and went outside to find it wasn't true. It was just a heterosexual couple having an argument outside. I went back into the social to find one of the organizers up on stage, making an announcement through the P.A. She said that the N.F were outside and trying to get in. She looked cold and mindless. I could see the panic on everyone's faces at this terrifying announcement. They all knew how violent the N.F were and how much they hated lesbians. I was blazing with anger at this totally irresponsible action, so I jumped up on the stage and spoke into one of the other mics.

'The N.F are not outside. There's a heterosexual couple having an argument and even they're gone now.'

'Why's she said the N.F are outside then?' a woman in the audience shouted up, indicating the organizer who'd made the announcement.

'I don't know but I can tell you I've been outside. I've checked the whole thing out myself and the N.F are definitely not out there,' I persisted. 'Just enjoy the rest of the night,' I said, trying to break a smile through the mayhem.

The rest of the social carried on without a hitch; it was once people started to walk home that the trouble started. There was an unnerving silence all through the air. Some woman had been attacked, smashed over the head with a truncheon, by a man in a dark-colored, combat-type jacket. Everyone knew it was the police. Suddenly, a rake of cops appeared from nowhere. They were standing in the street, shoulders back, looking very threatening. Some of them were in plain clothes instead of official uniforms and of course their plain clothes included, wait for it, wow what a coincidence, dark khaki combat jackets. Talk about brass fuckin' neck.

I absolutely shat myself trying to get out of the area in one piece - every step was a step further towards freedom. I saw an obviously injured woman lying in the street with another woman kneeling over her crying. There was a policeman in a combat jacket stood next to them and a policeman in uniform next to him. As I got nearer I could see the woman on the floor was Bette and there was a pool of blood on the ground next to her. The woman kneeling over her was Billie, her new girlfriend, a black woman who I was friends with. There was no way that I could have risked helping them. If I'd have gone anywhere near them, the police looked like they'd have smashed my head in as well. I knew they'd have to radio for an ambulance as that they couldn't let her die on the street, not with witnesses around anyway.

I found out the next day that they'd also attacked Alex and Amy from our street, smashing them over their heads as well. They too had to get their heads stitched. The incident earlier in the evening, with the heterosexual couple arguing outside the social, suddenly felt connected to this violent onslaught of police brutality. It all seemed a bit too coincidental to me. And who started the N.F rumor to make people panic and get outside, and probably have your head smashed in, earlier? No wonder they were called pigs.

Bette had seven stitches in her head and was in bed for a day or two to recover from her dreadful ordeal. I hadn't been in touch with her for what seemed like ages, but I rang the next day to see how she was and said I'd go over on Saturday to take her stitches out, so that she wouldn't have the hassle of going back to the hospital. She was very pleased that I'd phoned her again. So was I really; I missed her a lot.

When Saturday arrived, I was very anxious about venturing over to Brixton, as rioting had broken out on the Friday. It said on the news that things had calmed down and the rioting had actually stopped on Saturday morning. I was still worried about going but felt I had to as Bette's stitches needed to come out that day. Things didn't go well. The bus that I was travelling on had to stop outside the center of Brixton because the rioting had started off again. Everyone had to get off the bus and walk. It was a very hot, humid day, even though it was only April. You could have cut the atmosphere on the streets with a knife: I've never known such a feeling on every street around me. As I started to walk along the road ahead of me, there was a policeman standing in the middle of the street and unlike every other time you see the police, he had his eyes pointing down to the ground, like he was scared to look up. I thought, 'Well, this is a turn up for the books - a copper not being cocky, especially when there's so much going on. Nothing like last Saturday, when they were beating the shit out of everyone.' There was only a handful of people on the streets.

I wormed my way round each street and corner, nervous at what I might find every step of the way. I felt like I'd been dropped by the bus straight into a war zone. It had never occurred to me that the rioting would break out again, I thought that it had stopped for good. I'd hardly ever even heard of rioting, never mind been trapped in a friggin' riot zone. Jesus! The air was so hot and sticky. Electricity was waiting to strike out at any second, yet to unleash the flood of suffering from the mighty, heavy clouds that hung over Brixton.

I was a bit nervous of being out in these streets with my white skin, as the few people I did come across, in this deserted area, were all black. Yet I didn't meet with any animosity from anybody. As time went on I realized that I was far more nervous about bumping into the police than anything else. After walking for about a mile, I finally managed to get to Bette's house in Villa Road. What a relief. Bette had been out somewhere and was not long back. She beamed when she saw me standing at her door. We went downstairs to the basement

living room/kitchen and garden doors area. There
was a message chalked onto the communal
blackboard from one of her housemates - 'Feeling
twitchy? Wondering where everyone is? Lee xx'.
Bette smiled when she read it.

'Oh, look it's from Lee, she must've gone out. I
wonder what time she wrote that, I didn't see it
earlier 'cos I went upstairs,' Bette said.

'D'ya think she'll be alright?' I inquired, a bit
concerned.

'Yeah, she'll have gone down the road to
number 19's,' Bette nodded her head slightly to
one side.

I took Bette's seven stitches out and hung about
for a few hours in the hope of some news that the
rioting was over. Although I felt fairly safe in the
house, I also felt under siege. People kept popping
in and out with different local news bulletins.
Someone even said people were rioting right
outside the very house that we were in. Rumors
were rife, people were very jumpy, and to a degree
seemed to relish in the excitement of it all at the
same time.

When the rumors quietened down I phoned my
mate Jessie to see if she knew what was happening
with the tube trains, seeing as she lived near
Brixton tube station. Nobody knew what the buses
were doing, so the tube was my only option.

'Oh, fuck the tube Cecilia,' Jessie said to me
straight away. 'Stay over here. You can't miss one

of the most exciting nights Brixton's had in years, can you?'

I screamed laughing at her. She could always be relied upon to see the funny side in everything. I truly loved her. 'No, you're right. I can't miss it, can I?' I said, still laughing.

'Of course not dear. The black people of Brixton have finally got the bastard police on the run. At long fuckin' last, our day has come,' Jessie screamed laughing. There was only one Jessie Miller in the world, what a character.

'What about drink?' I said, then paused.

'What about drink dear? We can go to the off-licence when you get here,' Jessie said. 'What's the matter dear? Are you worried those nasty black people will attack you when you're in't off-licence?' she continued, taking the piss out of my Northern accent and laughing.

'Yeah, not just black people though. Any rioters and the police. People always go after the off-licence, don't they? Well, I would if I was them.'

We both screamed laughing again.

'Don't worry dear, me and Simone will 'escort' you when you get here and we can get pissed and see how the night develops,' Jessie chuckled. 'We could've been pissed by now if it wasn't for them fuckin' rioters forcing Gordon to close the pub!' she shouted down the phone. My stomach was starting to hurt from laughing at her mad ravings. I could hear Simone shouting and laughing in the background. Oh dear, I couldn't wait to get over and see them - they were like true family to me. I wiped my eyes from laughing and said goodbye.

I braved the streets again and made it to her house in Josephine Avenue. I was a regular visitor to her home, since her mad ex had moved out and Simone, another black woman who owned the house had moved back in after time away travelling. Jessie was a fairly tall, dark skinned, black woman. She was one of very few people who I thought looked good in glasses and her dress sense was terrific as well. She'd come over to this country from Guyana, in South America, as a kid. She decided to speak as posh as the Queen so people would take her seriously. She did speak posh an' all. She told me that she was the first black person to go to Essex University.

Simone bought the big house they lived in with money from a car accident. There had always been a steady trickle of women moving in and out of the house, from all different parts of the world. As well as the women who actually lived there, there were quite often travelling women, who would stay for anything from a day up to a few months, or even longer. Milly and Angela lived there for a while, but Jessie's mad ex made life in the house at the time hard for everyone to live peacefully, so they didn't stop for long.

There was all sorts of toing and froing throughout the night. Everyone was very excited with the potential drama of the riots, which from all accounts seemed to have calmed down a bit. We had the telly on the whole time so we could watch the news and find out what was happening. Me, Jessie and Simone ventured out once - that was to go to the off licence. It seemed to be one of the very few places that was still open. The Asian man serving was red in the face from trying to keep up with the heavy demand for alcohol. People seemed to be stocking up by buying cans and bottles by the dozen. Maybe they thought they'd be stuck indoors if the rioting kicked off again. There was a highly charged atmosphere inside and around the off licence; it almost felt like one wrong move from anybody would make it all erupt. People were rushing about their business so they could get home, or somewhere else off the streets. I wasn't so scared having Jessie and Simone to 'escort' me (as Jessie put it). I had been walking on my own earlier and besides, t'off-licence was only across the road from us.

The night passed without any more trouble on the streets. We stayed up until all hours as usual, drinking, smoking dope and sorting out the world's problems with whoever wanted to listen to us, or to join in if they wanted. Hardly anyone had as much to say as Jessie, Simone or me. All three of us had very strong opinions, not only on the world's problems, but also surrounding class, racism, sexism, homophobia - you name it, we'd talk about it. They both taught me a lot about world politics, things I'd had no idea about before. They wouldn't just tell me one side of it neither; I'd get the whole picture - every date, fact and figure possible. I was always fascinated by what they had to say. We used to laugh and laugh so much as well.

I didn't know Simone as well as I knew Jessie. I'd met Jessie before I moved down to London. Simone had been off travelling for well over a year and had been back for about six months. She was about the same height as Jessie, mixed race, and was slightly more casual and hippie-ish in her dress sense than Jessie or me. I would've liked to have dressed more like her really, although I usually don't like hippie clothes, but I could tell when they suited the person wearing them. Simone wore a headband around her Afro sometimes, in a bit of a Jimi Hendrix style.

Although Simone had been around the world travelling, like a lot of lesbians did, she could only afford it because of her car accident compensation. The other female travelers were from families with money to fund them. One or two worked, saved up for the fare, then found jobs when they got to where they travelled to. Women could stay in other women's houses for free all over the world, particularly in London where there were so many squats to stay in. We were always getting women coming over to our street, all year round. Usually they'd stay at Vicky and Alex's, mainly because they had more room but also because they were at home all day to doss around with them. Occasionally, we would get an over-spill of women from their house wanting to stay with us. Sometimes we would get women desperate to get away from Vicky and Alex's frequent mad goings-on.

We made friends with a group of Danish women who were staying with Vicky and Alex. They were really nice. As soon as they could, all four of them would be down at our house every evening. It was great to see them all lying against the wall on Hannah's bed, with blankets over them, watching Coronation Street with us. They were totally at home. One of them was an artist and loved looking at the pictures that Hannah had drawn. They said that we could go and live in Denmark if we wanted and that they would give Hannah work as an artist. Hannah was very keen to take up this offer, but I wouldn't go because at the time I was still embroiled in my crazy relationship with Kate and my heart wouldn't let me be so far away from her. I sometimes wonder what our lives would have been like if we'd gone.

On another occasion, we had three German women staying. They got on my nerves though, mostly because we had a set routine in our house that centered around us getting up and going to work, coming home, having our tea, doing whatever we fancied, then going to bed. One morning I got up to find a washing line erected all across one wall of the kitchen, which also dangled over the cooker and main cooking area. Not only that, but it was full of horrible-looking knickers and god knows what else. To top it all, no one could get near the cooker, or anything else they may have required, in order to eat, or drink for that matter. There were dishes filled with beans, pulses and water in the one tiny place that was not filled with their crap. No one had bothered to ask if it was okay to set up a washing line indoors - there was a perfectly adequate line in the back garden. I didn't mind the food soaking in the dishes so much, I was glad in a way that they were joining in to cook, but I was really fed up about the line.

'Them German women are gonna have to go. Look at the state of that,' I said, looking at their washing and then at Gemma when I got home in the evening. Gemma screamed laughing.

'We can't just chuck them out just 'cos they've hung a washing line up,' she said, still laughing.

'Yeah we can. I can't live like this. Fuckin' hippies,' I said, moving my head about.

Gemma was getting hysterical. She knew I was exaggerating my words to make her laugh more, but she also knew I was very fed up at the same time. One of the German women came downstairs and into the kitchen. She was small, fair and always pleasant. Not being one to hide my feelings that much, she knew from my face that I was fed up with her. She looked really hurt and anxious, and had only come into the kitchen to make us all our tea. I immediately felt awful and Gemma started laughing to show me up even further.

'Hiya,' I said, smiling at the German woman.

'I was going to cook so we can all eat. Do you want to eat? I am not knowing what you want now,' the poor German woman struggled on, trying to work out what was the matter with me.

'Oh look, I'm really sorry, it's just this washing line up here,' I said, looking up at all their clothes on the line. 'You see we're out at work all day and when we get home we need space to cook. I can't cope with this washing line taking over the whole place. We put our washing outside to dry.' I smiled and looked towards the window at the top of the glass doors. 'I'm sorry for looking so stressed at you. I didn't mean to offend you,' I said, smiling again.

'No, you haven't offended me. I can understand this, I too have worked in Germany.' She put her head down then lifted it up.

'Have you?' I said, wide eyed and smiling,

'Yes, don't worry. I will tell the other woman to take down the line,' she said, then paused. 'We can cook for most days while we are here, if you would like us to. But I will understand if you want us to leave,' she said, looking up at me.

'No, no I don't want you to leave. It's fine. It would be lovely for you to cook and we will cook for you as well.' I beamed and put my hand on her shoulder. I was relieved that the air was cleared and we could all live peacefully in this house that was far too small for six adults.

One of the other German women was tall, blonde and quite attractive. A few nights after the air was cleared over the washing line, me, Hannah and the three Germans had all been chatting in the living room. After most people had gone to bed there was just me and the attractive German left in the living room that was adjoining my bedroom. I thought that maybe she wanted to shag me, guessing this from the way that all three of them suddenly started talking German just before the others went to bed. Although I couldn't tell what they were saying from their language, I could pick up a bit of what was going on. I suppose I was very familiar these days with body language and sexual vibes! We chatted a bit longer and although she was attractive and sexy looking, I didn't want to have sex with her. At this particular time in my life, before anything happened with this woman, I had begun to feel a bit harassed by women wanting to have sex with me. It was starting to take over my life too much. If it had been more plain sailing and women were as keen for my mind as they were for my body, then maybe I wouldn't have felt like this so much.

'All alone in such a big bed,' the sexy, seductive German woman said.

'Yes,' I smiled back at her. She was fine with me when I explained to her how I felt about everything. If it had been at a different time in my life, I know for sure we would have had horny, horny sex....

A few weeks after the police had been on their blood-thirsty lesbian, head smashing rampage, some of us organized a fund-raiser at the Drill Hall, off Tottenham Court Road, to help pay the victims' legal fees. There was a massive turnout in this big venue - bands played, women sang and there was meant to be an act whereby a woman came down from the high ceiling on some kind of a cable and onto the floor. She couldn't do it though, because there were too many people there, which was a bit disappointing because it looked like it would be brilliant to me. I loved any kind of circus-style act, especially daring ones that came down from the roof. Wow, just the thought of it thrills me.

After all the other acts had finished and there were just a few of us organizers left and bands packing up, the daredevil cable woman said she'd do her act for us, now there were less people around. She must've seen the thrill on my face when she said it and to my absolute joy she asked me if I wanted to do it instead of her.

'It's really straight-forward and very safe,' she said.

I didn't have time to let myself be scared of the height of it, so I shimmied up the ladder like a true trapeze artist, high up in the magical world of the big top, where all the bright lights shone down onto my awaiting audience. The daredevil cable woman came up the ladder with me and helped me get into place. I looked down at where I was going to land, then before I could think any further, that was it. Lift off! I held my head high and what a fucking brilliant time did I have whizzing down that wire. Words can't describe it. I felt like I'd waited all my life for this very moment. So much for the police trying to kill Lesbian spirit - it was a fantastic end to a fantastic night. Long may we reign.

Escape from Alkie Dad

Dad had been to visit us a couple of times since him and Mam had split up. Course he thought he'd died and gone to heaven, with the endless stream of women everywhere we went. At times, throughout his final visit, I began to wish he'd drop dead and go to hell. I was sick of people coming up to me in the pub, after they'd had their arms around his shoulder and saying to me and Hannah, 'Ahh, your Dad's dead nice int 'e?' People just laughed when I told them what an old creep he was. All they could see was him there with all the lesbians, and their Dad wasn't and probably never would be. I knew his visits would start to get more and more regular. Not only was there all this totty, and no other men around to compete with, but also we were in the pub all the time. All his dreams in one place, and two daughters to carry him home at the end of his pissed-up madness, every fuckin' night. Like I wasn't sick to the back teeth of having to do that for years on end as it was.

It was probably two months later, but felt more like two weeks after his last visit, that we heard he was in London visiting a young straight woman we knew from Lancaster who now lived down here. I was in the kitchen with Jill, Janet (my other mate from Bradford) Mari and Lucy from number 46 (who Mari had started seeing) and Hannah. Jill, Janet and me were off out on the town, Mari (who now lived with us since Gemma had moved out) and Lucy were going round to Lucy's, and Hannah was staying in for the night. Apart from Hannah, we were all just about to leave the house when we heard a loud knock on the door. Hannah and I must've looked terrified at each other.

'It's 'im. It's Dad. 'Es 'ere!' I hissed really loudly at Hannah. Hannah was always jumpy and easily scared at the best of times, I was the laid back one, but now even I was scared. I don't know why I was scared of that old bastard. The door banged even louder.

'Let's go and see if it's him through the cellar window,' Hannah said to me. We both dashed next door to the cellar and stared up through the window, shielded a bit by the metal gate. We could see this tall dark figure in a mad, long coat through the evening light.

I silently screamed to myself, 'It's 'im.' I hissed and shook my head wildly. We both ran back into the kitchen and quickly shut the door behind us.

'It's me Dad, he's 'ere,' I whispered loudly to the others waiting in the kitchen. They were all grinning, with slightly confused looks on their faces at the same time. Not knowing or daring to ask what was going to happen.

'What we gonna do?' Hannah asked me, starting to panic.

'He's not coming in. I'm not having him in here again, not after last time,' I said, shaking my head and stressing out.

'We can't just leave him standing outside,' Hannah said, waving her arms out towards the cellar. The knocking got louder and louder.

'Yes we can. I don't want him in this house,' I said, starting to raise my voice.

'I can't cope with this, I've got to let him in,' Hannah said, really flappin' now.

The others in the room kept looking at me, then at Hannah as each one of us spoke, our voices getting louder and louder all the while.

'No. Because if you let him in it'll be me that has to speak to him, and me who has to sort everything out,' I said, waving my arms in the air.

Bang! Bang! Bang!

'How much fuckin' louder could he bang on the friggin' door?' I thought to myself.

'Right, I'm going to let him in, I can't stand it anymore,' Hannah said, moving towards the door.

'You open that door and I'm off over the backs,' I said, staring at Hannah, then glancing at Jill and Janet to make sure that they were ready for our quick exit. Mari and Lucy looked up ready for their getaway as well.

Hannah opened the kitchen door.

'Right, come on. We're off,' I said, tuning to Jill and Janet. They followed swiftly behind me, as did Mari and Lucy. All five of us raced past Hannah, as she stood still holding the kitchen door open, and hot footed it up the stairs and out the back. We climbed over next door's wall, through their garden and into Lucy's, where we slipped through to the next street without him seeing us.

I found out later that when Hannah let him in she told him that he couldn't stay. She said he was fine about it, gave her a tenner and then went off to stay with the straight woman from Lancaster again. I was very surprised that she stood up to him. It was about time that she started to stand up to people more. Who better to start with than him?

We always had a constant stream of visitors from various places up north, the main one was our Bernie. Despite her coming down to stay on a regular basis I missed her quite a lot really. She and I lived in the same house in Lancaster for a couple of years; Kate lived with us for about six months until we two got our own place. I used to worry that Bernie would be lonely after me, Kate and Hannah moved down here. She'd write joint letters to me and Hannah and we wrote joint letters back. Me and Hannah were a bit inseparable, not even writing separate letters to people. We even had an agreement between us, that whenever we went out with our girlfriends at night, we would try to make sure that we came back to our house, rather than going to theirs, so that we could be together. We never told any of our girlfriends that we had this arrangement; it would only cause stupid jealousies from their side if we had. Most women liked our strong connection. It was just the odd silly ones that didn't, and even so, I still think most of them wouldn't have liked our arrangement if they knew about it.

Bernie would sometimes address our joint letters to include Gemma as well. All three of us would sit around the kitchen table while Hannah or I read her letter out loud. Occasionally there would be other people around who hadn't even met Bernie, sitting down and listening to her news and mad goings on.

One time when she'd been down for a couple of weeks, she started to miss male company towards the end of the second week. There were a few of us playing pool and chatting and I could tell there was something on her mind just from her body language. She seemed a bit awkward when I asked her what was up with her. She looked over at a group of smart, good-looking black men playing pool on the table next to us, who weren't regulars. At first, I wondered if they had said something horrible to her and was half getting ready for a fight. When I looked at them, one of them smiled back, really friendly.

'Stop, stop looking at him,' Bernie said anxiously.

'What? I'm not doing anything,' I said, grinning at her. I knew she fancied them then.

'I know what you're like,' she said, laughing. 'Don't you dare say anything. I mean it,' she continued, half laughing and half trying to get mad with me, in case I showed her up.

'Go on, I promise I won't say 'owt. D'ya fancy them?' I said, moving away from the dykes, so they couldn't hear.

'It's not that so much - I'm just starting to miss male company.' She paused. 'I don't want all you to think I don't like female company, by wanting to be with men as well.' She looked awkward.

'Don't be daft. You're a straight woman, you're bound to want to be with straight men as well as us. Fuckin' hell, imagine if I was with just men for two whole weeks. I'd be desperate to be with women. Jesus.' I shook my head and Bernie beamed.

'Shall I go and talk to them?' I said, looking over towards the men.

'No, don't you dare,' Bernie said.

I sidled over to the men's pool table. The one who had beamed at me earlier came right round the table to greet me, with a pool cue still in his hand.

'Hi,' he said, smiling.

I could see Bernie squirming, terrified of what I'd say to him. I put my arm around her.

'Hiya. I was just wondering if you'd fancy a game of pool with us. My sister's been down visiting and she hasn't had any male company for two weeks,' I said, smiling and glancing at Bernie. We both started laughing.

'Yeah, yeah, sure - we'd love a game,' the man said.

'You see, I'm not bothered myself but Bernie is a bit,' I said.

Bernie started laughing at me and shaking her head. He and his mates stayed over with us, chatting and playing pool for the rest of the night.

It wasn't too long before Bernie started seeing Dirck, a Dutch man she had met in Lancaster. She'd often stop over with us on her way to see him. It was just a matter of time before she decided to move over to live with him. She had her suitcase all packed and ready to leave from our house to start her new life in Holland. We stayed up chatting the night before she was due to leave, with Hannah and I saying to her what a great time she'd have over there but she was nervous about such a big move. Early the next morning, she was still a bit worried about going. I carried her suitcase out to the front doorstep where Hannah was standing waiting for her to finally leave. It was all a bit sad and tense as our kid was moving to another country. I lifted the suitcase down off the step and onto the pavement and as soon as it hit the ground, the entire contents burst out onto the street. All three of us got absolutely hysterical laughing and suddenly the seriousness of this sad moment was totally overturned into something light and comical. It was a great send off for her.

Since I'd become a gardener, for the first time in my entire life I actually had a bit of time to myself. All the while when I was growing up, I hardly got a minute to even have a private thought, never mind anything else. It still did my head in at home though, with the constant visitors, phone calls, band practices et cetera. More and more, people treated our house like some kind of HQ. It was starting to annoy me as time went by, like it did when I was a teenager with Mam's open door policy that let 'every dog and divil' into our hospitable house. Just as it had been then, I didn't want to be spread so thinly. At least Mam listened when I was finally the eldest in the home, and said she understood that I didn't want the old lady round the corner coming for Christmas. Just for once I wanted it to be family and nobody else. It was bad enough there being so many of us as it was, without having to give time to others. I was sick of it then and was getting sick of it now, not to mention the fact that people made such annoying presumptions about me.

There was the constant class war that was forever raging inside my head, and outside of it for that matter. Hardly anyone ever wanted to discuss my working-class politics, and they would run a mile rather than speak to me seriously, or even casually for that matter. Meanwhile, they could be free to patronize me and put me down at their leisure. The only brief respite I ever got was with Charlie (the woman from Bradford that Ruth got into a relationship with) after we'd got to be best mates, and of course when I went over to Josephine Avenue in Brixton. That was a godsend to me, the release of going over there. It got to the stage that I would spend almost every weekend in Brixton. When I was there I felt like I didn't have to keep fighting for my very existence.

I met a whole new community when I was with Jessie and Simone which was very refreshing compared to the unchanging Stepney. Most of the visible lesbian scene was white and middle class, so had a bit of a blinkered outlook on the world. As far as I could see, they didn't have a scrap of politics between them. They'd lived this sheltered life until they got to university when, shock horror, they discovered oppression not only as women, but also in the shape of their sexuality. Yippidee-doo, we can play at being political too. Keep the cotton wool on though, stay in the comfort zone, and show little or no allegiance to other far more oppressed people than themselves. The general line on women's politics was that because we are all women, we are all equally oppressed. That was the biggest pile of shite I'd ever heard, totally going against any form of equality whatsoever.

The message being if you're not white, English, middle class and able-bodied, then you can fuck off.

Since the working classes had been recognized as having existence in this country, no one had ever seemed to take their plight seriously. Sadly, the only group of people that seemed to include them in anything were the National Front, fuckin' fascists. I gave up bothering to have any form of political discussion with most of the people I met. Despite a lot of them having degrees, and a supposedly 'good education', they didn't have enough upstairs to join in a decent conversation on any level. The irony was that in their eyes I was supposed to be the thick, working class person who knew nothing.

Women who saw themselves at the top of the right-on, politically aware, purity ladder would quite often be the worst in their oppressive attitudes - laughing when they heard my accent, not listening when I spoke my views and opinions. One woman who had been joint top of the 'lesbian ladder' in Lancaster, who had now returned to London, referred to my mate Jessie as 'black Jessie'. She thought nothing of it either, that was until she saw the look on my face as my jaw dropped, and even then, she was only slightly uncomfortable.

No one seemed to put their money where their mouth was; it was all words and too little action for my liking. One time Hannah and I were at a club called Kaine's, somewhere between King's Cross and Islington, with Vicky and Alex and some other women. It was mostly women, with just a few men allowed in. This particular night there was a drag act on - a gay man dressed up as a woman and supposedly acting like one as well. Vicky and Alex decided to instigate some direct action, and got some of us to boo him off. Penny, the owner, was furious. Vicky and Alex stood arguing the odds with her. 'This degrades women,' I heard them say. I totally agreed and found it all far more entertaining than his stupid act anyway. But then what got me was a few weeks later, at another mixed and much bigger event, Alex was up dancing all bloody night with a man in drag and done up to the nines in makeup. She was raving on about how she loved queens. Again, what was all that about? Wishy washy words that barely warranted any political credibility.

This was a long way from the guts and passion I witnessed when I went over to see Jessie and Simone at my weekend home in Brixton. One time I had a really rotten cold and had decided to stay at home and not go over like I usually did. I had already told Jessie on the Thursday that I wasn't going over, but by Saturday morning she was on the phone to Hannah while I was still in bed.

'Tell Cecilia to get her arse over here. She can't not come over just for a bloody cold,' was the message relayed back to me.

'Oh god, what's she like?' I said, laughing when Hannah told me. I got up out of bed, then an hour later the phone rang again. I knew that it'd be Jessie and I also knew it would be no good trying to resist her comical persuasion.

'Cecilia you fool, where the fucking hell are you?' Jessie said to me, then burst out laughing.

I started laughing then said, 'I've got a bad cold you maniac, I'm all sweaty.'

'You're all sweaty Betty. Oh, don't be such a wuss. When has a cold ever stopped me from drinking?' Jessie continued. I couldn't argue with anything ever stopping Jessie from having a drink, that was for sure. 'I've already made us a chicken curry. That'll help you sweat it out a bit more,' Jessie said, knowing full well that food was always my weakness, and that her chicken curry was my absolute favorite dish of all time. I could feel her deliberately being quiet while she waited for her powers of persuasion to work on me. It was almost like a standoff between us. I knew as soon as she said those magic words, 'chicken curry', that there was no point in trying to fight her, so off I went back over to Brixton. So much for will power, or should I say curry that worked like a medicine on me.

The social scene in Brixton in south London was quite different to the one north of the river. For one, black women had more of a voice and weren't treated as if they were invisible as they often were on the rest of the women's scene. I preferred the music as well, to the other scenes, but best of all for me was the massive contrast in political opinions.

My parents were immigrants to this country, just as most of the black women's parents were, and this gave me a bit of an allegiance with them, something that was totally missing with the rest of the women on the scene. However, there were still quite a few white women around on the Brixton scene - most of them seemed to be fairly aware of their surroundings and more respectful of people in general. I was genuinely shocked on one occasion though, when I brought one of my white working-class friends and her girlfriend over to a women's disco at South London Women's Centre in Brixton. She had met Jessie through me already and always had a really good laugh with her, which is why I brought them both along. Neither of them had ventured across the river much previously, despite both being born and bred in London. My friend was like a fish out of water; I couldn't work her out. She'd always given me the impression that she was really hot on working-class beliefs and politics, and here she was, freaking out because there were more black women at the disco than white. When I asked her what was wrong with her, she said that all the black women were deliberately ignoring her. I was puzzled by this horrible reaction.

'Have you said hello or spoke to anyone yourself?' I asked.

'No, no I haven't,' she said, looking really uncomfortable and getting ready to leave.

'Well why not? You're usually friendly with everyone. What's up with ya?' I said, hurt and disappointed with her. I had never seen this strange side before.

'What about Jessie?' I said, pausing.

'What about Jessie?' she said, also pausing.

'Are you gonna tell her why you're leaving?' I persisted, looking straight into her eyes, hoping that she would say it was all a big misunderstanding and she didn't mean it.

'No, I don't know where she is," she said, looking towards the floor.

'She's in there, with everyone else,' I nodded towards the main part of the disco. I knew there was no way she would go in to say goodbye. I was starting to get really pissed off with her now.

'Look, we're just going to go. We never should've come over in the first place,' she said, starting to move towards the door.

'No, you're right - you never should've come over. I wish I'd never asked you.'

Ruby was a local West Indian woman who lived in Brixton, near Jessie and Simone. She was a bit older than us, probably in her early forties. Like a lot of women of her generation, she couldn't quite bring herself to saying that she was a lesbian, always referring to herself as bisexual. Who could blame her? It was hard enough for us younger women to be out lesbians as it was. Ruby had been around the Brixton community for years longer than any of us; maybe she was cautious of being ostracized for daring to be too different. There was a lot of homophobia within the black community as well as with white people. One night a group of West Indian men stood outside a house where a lesbian party was going on. They shouted at the women inside demanding that they 'give them back their women', referring to the black lesbians inside. They just got laughed at and soon disappeared, thankfully.

Ruby was quite intrigued with Jessie and Simone and me when we spent time with her. She'd sit in the George Canning pub with us and our circle of friends and talk to us for hours on end, in between flitting around the pub chatting with everyone else in this large, friendly watering hole. I don't think she'd met one openly out lesbian before, never mind a whole crowd of us. The first time I met her was in the pub. She came and sat right next to me, then proceeded to gently stroke my shoulder and upper arm, totally uninvited I might add. She said how strong I was and how much she liked it. Woowff! I think I might have blushed slightly - Jessie and Simone thought it was hilarious of course. I liked her but not in the way she wanted me to. After a few weeks she gave up trying to seduce me and we got on a lot better. She opened up a women-only blues night in either her cellar or someone else's. I loved late-night blues cellar sessions but they weren't exactly welcoming to lesbians, so this was perfect for me. Sadly Ruby's didn't last for long, which was a shame because it could've been a nice little earner for her as well as being a brilliant night out for us.

One night, me and Jessie went out quite late looking to buy some drink. It must've been about 2am. It wasn't like us to run out of alcohol I might add. I wasn't sure where, if anywhere, we would get something to drink at this time of night. That didn't seem to matter though - we were on a mission strolling around the streets of Brixton to see what we could come up with. Jessie was like a sniffer dog, checking out every nook and cranny on each street we walked down. It wasn't long before we came across a small Rasta man standing outside a house. We got chatting with him and discovered that he ran a regular blues night in the basement of his home. It was still 'early' so the music wasn't going to start till about 3 or 4. He said that we could come in and get some drink from inside to take away. When we walked through to the basement, I was really surprised at the huge number of cans of Red Stripe, stacked almost to the ceiling next to the massive speakers which stood nearly as high. What a result for us. Not just a teeny weenie chance of a few cans somewhere but a feast-your-eyes mountain of booze. We couldn't believe it. This Rasta chap was genuinely pleased to meet us and kept laughing at Jessie's witticisms and he insisted on giving us the cans for free. We thanked him, said our goodbyes and then set off back to Josephine Avenue where Simone and some others were waiting for our boozy booty.

On a hot Saturday evening in the George Canning Pub, me, Jessie, Simone and quite a few others, including Shamim, Gemma's recent ex, were in chatting and having a laugh like we did. Ruby came over and joined us, as did this youngish, white, middle-class man who nobody knew. He just sat on the edge of our crowd and started chatting to us. He seemed inoffensive at first, but it wasn't long before he started coming out with homophobic and racist rhetoric, thinly disguised as 'just liberal discussion', as he so stupidly put it. Things suddenly got very messy. Our entire table turned on him, all except Ruby that is, who in her niceness wanted to give him the benefit of the doubt. I think she mistakenly thought we were being horrible to him because he was a man on his own, and perhaps because we were lesbians as after all, we must be man-haters (daft ideology). Things turned from bad to worse and the nasty little shit ended up having to leave before he got chucked out. We all gave a collective sigh of relief once the freakin' fascist left and we settled back into our seats. The next thing we knew, a fucking brick exploded through the massive window right behind us like a bomb. It sent big sheets of glass crashing down on us. Suddenly everything around me went into slow motion as I sat in total shock, unable to take in the magnitude of this horrific scene. By the grace of God, as my Mam would say, nobody got hurt. It could've been carnage with the number of huge pieces of glass flying around. Me and Shamim were the only ones touched by it and even then, it was only a speck of blood.

Happy Go-Lucky

Although I spent a lot of weekends in Brixton I still liked to go out north of the river as well; despite white middle class women being in the majority there were still some women from all over the world out and about. One such woman was Thea a tall, skinny, dark, Greek woman who had some very playful and sexy ways about her. She was good looking and not quite as feminine as most of the women that I fancied. I hadn't had a girlfriend for about three months after Bette and I split up, apart from one-nighters here and there. I suppose that I was still fed up with people not seeing me properly for who I was. If it wasn't for such strong sexual desires that constantly surged through my whole body, then I doubt I would've even had the one-night stands.

Thea was usually with a crowd of other Greek women whenever I saw her. They were always laughing, dancing and generally looked like they were having a good time. The first time I encountered them was at a women's art alliance disco at Regent's Park. There were one or two of them in the group that were quite fanciable, as well as Thea, but Thea was the one I fancied most. She had a girlfriend called Annabel, a young, dark-haired, blue-eyed, pretty English rose who always looked off her face on booze whenever I saw her. This girlfriend had a girlfriend, so I knew that Thea would probably be free to have another as well. Every time Thea saw me she would always manage to touch me somewhere or another, even if she was dancing intimately with Annabel. I knew she wanted me - my body was desperate to devour her very being each time she touched or toyed with it...

If either Hannah or I really fancied someone, then we'd send the other one on a mission to find out all about them, the main thing being to establish what our chances of shagging them were. I asked Hannah if she would 'go fishing' for me, see how things stood with the sexy Thea. Hannah hadn't even had the chance to start her investigations when, three days after I'd asked her, the phone went and lo and behold it was Thea. She'd managed to get my number off somebody and here she was, asking if I'd like to go over to her house in Kensington, of all posh places. I couldn't believe my luck. She wanted me there the next day, no messing, and of course I was more than happy to oblige.

I loved my daytime dates, mmm...

Sunshine. Clean body ready to get dirty. Fresh clothes wrapping themselves around every smoldering inch of it.

I was a wild, big cat slowly prowling from room to room, as I got ready to leave the house and go over to savor the fruits of my long awaiting body. She'd pawed and toyed with me for long enough. I wanted to throw my head back and roar and roar, like the wild beast that I felt I was through my entire soul and body. She'd already picked up my scent, by phoning me so soon after I sent it out. East End was about to meet West End.

The sun was shining on the grey flats of the concrete jungle as I stepped out into the street. It was no place for a lion like me to be on the loose. I needed fresher air and more open space. The caged bus to Aldgate led me to the Circle Line tube station where I turned into a snake that slowly wound its way round to the Central line, the line that was bright red and went like an artery from east to west. I shed the snake's skin and stepped onto the long train. The big cat was back, but now she was a cheetah - lithe, ripe and ready for action.

As soon as Thea opened her front door she looked thrilled to see me. She put her arms around my neck and put her hand on my chest.

'Cec', she said, looking straight into my eyes. 'You came all the way to see me.' She held both my hands and smiled and smiled. I loved this big continental open display of affection.

'Yes, I did.' I said, smiling shyly.

'Come in, come in.' She kept hold of one of my hands and led me through the door. She lived in a huge rented flat with about three other Greek women. I liked the feel of her house. It was warm and inviting. She said that all the other women were off out in the sunshine. I didn't mind missing out on the beautiful day, seeing as I was here at long last with the delicious Thea. I wanted to devour her straight away, but managed to keep my wild desires down to a deep, silent purr.

We walked through the flat and into her spacious, sexy bedroom. She sat me on her bed while she went off and got me some juice, then came back and sat right down beside me. We talked and laughed together for about two or three hours. She showed me pictures of Greece and paintings, poems, beads, bangles, jewelry. She told me stories to go with them. I absolutely loved being with her. It was so refreshing to share her enthusiasm for her culture and her love of life. I'd found out so much about her in such a short space of time.

Much as we'd have both loved to talk forever, the serious business of what we both knew I was there for couldn't be kept down for any longer. I'd been very aware of her every move. Each time she'd brush her body next to mine, I had to stop it from screaming out for her and surging forward, desperate to devour her. We'd stayed on the bed the whole time I'd been there, which made all our interactions so far seem like lustful foreplay. I was so turned on, it was getting harder and harder to keep any kind of eye contact with her. As usual I was desperate for her to make the first move. The conversation finally ended, to reveal a deep, deep, sexual tension between us, our eyes locked together. She kept my gaze and put her hand on my belt and untied it very slowly. I was totally hooked into her; who am I to resist such wild Greek passions?

We spent the whole weekend shagging. And the next one. And the one after that. It was wild, unadulterated lust. The other Greek women in the flat called in to say hello the odd time, not bothering to knock half the time I might add. How many Greek women in one weekend can see me not only naked, but also in the middle of having sex?

By the third weekend Thea's girlfriend had started ringing while I was there, not just once but a few times. She had finished with her other woman and wanted Thea's shoulder to cry on. As soon as I heard that she'd ended that relationship a little alarm bell rang deep inside of me. I didn't take much notice of it because I was so engrossed in having sex with Thea. I felt like I was on a beautiful, magical journey with her. I'd never had a lover that gripped my imagination so much.

Thea came to stay with me in Stepney. I remember being embarrassed when she asked me where she should go to use the toilet in the night. We had a bucket outside the upstairs bedrooms

and an old-fashioned pot in the downstairs in case
we didn't want to go outside in the middle of the
night for a wee. She was the only person who
seemed put out at having to use a bucket to piss in.
It wasn't the nicest thing to have to do I must say,
but needs must. I somehow smoothed over it and
pretended that we didn't really use a bucket to piss
in, honest. I suppose Greece wasn't freezing like
this country and maybe the threat of weirdos
hanging about the area while you ran outside half-
naked wasn't too much of an issue there either.

Once, when my bedroom was downstairs, I
woke up very early one glorious summer's day and
saw Juno, one of Gemma's girlfriends, walking
from the toilet to the back door. She was
completely naked; the sun shining all over her
beautiful body. As I watched this heavenly vision
of beauty pass right by my window I literally and
metaphorically saw Juno in a completely different
light from that moment on.

A six-week trip back to Greece had been
planned by Thea. She knew I couldn't get so much
time off work when she told me about it but she
seemed frustrated that I couldn't just up sticks and
go like she could. As the time got nearer for her to
go, she started spending most of her week with
Annabel. I mostly only saw her at weekends unless
she came over to mine when I came back to bed
after I'd clocked in at work. I knew her girlfriend
was freaked out by Thea's closeness to me; she

was forever ringing while I was visiting her. I
didn't want to know what was going on with them.
Annabel seemed like a spoilt brat to me, seething
and bemused that 'her' girlfriend would find some
working-class northerner like me attractive. She
seemed to think that she was perfectly cool and
beautiful, totally ignoring the fact that she was fast
becoming a bad alcoholic and letting her whole
soul and personality be consumed by it.

The two of them trotted off to Greece together,
Thea promising me that she would write and ring
me, and she would miss me, and my sweet, sweet,
body. She did write a couple of letters, and she
phoned me one early Saturday morning, when I
was still asleep in bed. Because I was still half
asleep I couldn't muster up the enthusiasm for her
call. She was pissed off that I wasn't jumping for
joy at the sound of her voice. I could almost feel
the end of our relationship there and then.
Although I missed her in the six weeks that she
was away, I still carried on living my life to the
full, as much as I usually did. Again, literally and
metaphorically, I didn't let the grass grow. Lawns
had to be mowed, flower beds weeded and dug
over, pool needed to be played with the chaps from
work. Grace, my youngest sister, came to visit and
last but not least, other women wanted me.

I'd been at Jessie and Simone's after the pub.
They had a tall, blonde, short haired, very
voluptuous Dutch woman staying with them. I'd

seen her getting into bed in the living room downstairs when I'd come back in to get my shoes - she was naked and nicely tanned all over. She smiled deep into my eyes.

'Are you wanting to sleep here?' she asked me, looking at the space next to her. Suddenly it wasn't all Greek to me anymore and I was filled with passionate Dutch courage. She pulled the covers back so I could see her sexy, sexy, naked body - my whole body screamed with delight. I whipped my clothes off in seconds. There was no time for talking. Lust lurched me forward and I slid in next to her. She put her arms around me and pulled me into her.

The Friday after Thea and the alky got back from Greece, I was invited over to meet Thea and some of her friends in the pub in nearby Holland Park. It was a million miles away from Stepney. The streets were clean and leafy, little houses dotted about the place, huge mansion-size houses stood in small grounds. Wealth was in your face everywhere. I'd assumed that Thea was going to be in the pub with her house mates, having a welcome back home drink. I was looking forward to seeing them outside of the flat for a change. But when I got there it was a different story.

The pub was fairly busy on this late summer evening. I couldn't see where Thea and her merry band were when I first arrived so I stood at the bar waiting to get served. I was always confident when

I went out; it didn't faze me that the other customers could well be some of the richest people in the land. Mam always taught me that I was as good as everybody else and better than most. Besides, I'd wiped the arses of more aristocracy when I was nursing at St. Thomas' than I care to remember. A face is a face and an arse is an arse. They're all the bloody same in my book. They all need love and care, no matter who they belong to.

I waited patiently to be served. I became mesmerized by the many mirrors behind the bar. The low sunlight sparkled over them, and seemed like they were the entrance to the hall of mirrors in a circus or fairground, enticing you in to see who knows what. Amidst all the shimmering and twinkling colors, reflecting to show me what was going on behind me, I suddenly spotted Thea and her Grecian entourage through one of the mirrors, sitting at a table. My heart did a little summersault when I first saw her. A split second later I saw that clown of an alky girlfriend in another mirror. What a fool she was, sat there like a ventriloquist's dummy moving her eyes from side to side and her wooden mouth up and down, with her nasty streak clearly visible. My instinct told me to leave there and then, even before Thea spotted me. I suppose that I naturally assumed that Thea wanted to see me and the alky was just leaving. Fat chance.

I got my drink and made my way over to their table. Thea was thrilled to see me but was worried.

It was obviously because silly Annabel was still hanging about. As soon as I saw her I could tell that she was well on her way to being pissed out of her head, despite it only being 8 o'clock in the evening. She looked up at me with a stupid sardonic smile, her lips curling in on themselves as she made no attempt to hide her seething hatred of me.

Like a lot of alkies, she was good at hiding just how pissed up she really was. I could spot it straight away though, as soon as I saw the gleam in her puppet's eyes, when she wrapped her arms around her pint of lager, glass of wine and a Bloody Mary (vodka and tomato juice) like they were her long lost children. Suddenly it all seemed a bit too sinister for my liking and for the other Greek women, who looked very uncomfortable when they saw me walking over to their table. They'd smiled, made their apologies and left. I knew the tense atmosphere was because the 'girlfriend' was being drunk and obnoxious; I could see it written on everyone's faces as soon as I saw them. Although I was pleased to see Thea I felt a massive barrier had been built around her and I couldn't get near. She became a bit distant from me and distracted. She didn't seem too bothered by the drunken bad atmosphere. She was probably well used to it, having just spent six whole weeks with her. I, on the other hand, hated obnoxious drunks. The girlfriend started immediately to verbally attack me - blathering on about the working classes, trying to dress her hatred and snobbery up as some kind of sick pseudo intellectualism. I wouldn't rise to her pathetic games; I just kept batting her stupidity back at her. Thea, in her naïve liberalism, was actually taking her nastiness seriously and half expected me to go along with it. Maybe she was desperate for someone else to try and appease the nasty little shit.

'Annabel doesn't want to leave, she was supposed to go earlier,' Thea said to me like it was okay for all three of us to be together, and worst still, it was okay for the nasty little shit to be attacking me constantly.

I should've just left there and then, but agreed to go back to the flat. Thea said that Annabel had to pick up some things she left in the flat, and then she would go. Of course, she didn't just go. She wanted to carry on drinking when we arrived back in the flat. Thea asked me if it was okay if Annabel stayed longer, to have another drink. I could only look in disbelief and shake my head as Annabel cracked open a bottle of wine and started to pour the contents into a glass, grinning as she did so. That smug, stupid grin was the last straw and my cue to leave. I'd had enough and told Thea I was going home. She walked to the bedroom door with me and held my hand as I paused to leave. She looked into my eyes.

'Cec,' she paused, 'I have bought you a present from my country', she said pulling on my heart strings. She handed me a beautiful necklace that sparkled with love and care. I looked deep into her eyes, then over at her bed, totally ignoring the drunken pig sat nearby. Thea looked at the bed too and stroked my face really gently.

'Listen, I'll phone you tomorrow,' I said softly, then turned to leave. I carried on seeing Thea for only a short time after that night, which was a shame because I loved being with her.

Now my attention went back to my family. Bernie was due on a visit from Holland where she had settled with her lover and we were thrilled she was coming. Grace was coming down from the North at the same time. All four of us loved getting together; each one counting the weekends till we'd meet up. Hannah and Mari's band had a big women-only gig on the Saturday night in Covent Garden, which our sisters would be here for. I invited Jessie and Simone. Jessie had met 'the girls' quite a few times before - she always said, 'our Bernie' or 'our Grace' when she referred to them just to make me laugh. Simone didn't know them as well as Jessie did, but she was still delighted to be invited out on the town with us. It was wonderful for me to be going out with not only my closest sisters, but also my closest friends.

The weekend was finally here - whoopee! Bernie and Grace arrived on the Friday night and there was such a light, happy atmosphere in the house. I was first up on the Saturday morning so after I'd made everyone a cup of tea, I went round the corner to get bagels for breakfast from the Jewish bakery. We spent the whole morning just laughing and laughing, at long last catching up with each other. Hannah was to meet Mari and the others at the gig venue at about two o'clock for a sound check, so all of us got ready and set off for Covent Garden with her. While the band had their sound check, the rest of us had a mooch about the buzzing atmosphere of Covent Garden's trendy shops and open-air stalls. There were buskers, dancers, break-dancers, jugglers, you name it and it was here at Covent Garden, all in the open air. The sun was shining and it felt really good to be alive.

Jessie and Simone met us at the Naz on Brick Lane, early that evening.

'We nearly got fucking lost dear,' Jessie said to me in her posh voice, when she finally managed to get herself sat down at our long table in the Naz. 'Of course, it was Simone's fault', Jessie flicked her hand towards Simone. I laughed into my glass of water. Simone saw me laughing from across the table.

'Eh, what's she saying about me? She's the one who said she knew the way', Simone said laughing and throwing her arms up in the air. Jessie couldn't keep a straight face for much longer and joined in with the whole table laughing.

After we finished our delicious curry, all seven of us headed back to Covent Garden for the highlight of the evening - Hannah singing and playing lead guitar in her band. She was fantastic. It really added to her performance, Bernie and Grace being there, cheering her on. I loved the songs they sang; Hannah and Mari wrote most of them. Songs of lesbian love-making, songs of being working class and on the dole, 'Pool Fever' a song about playing pool with a cocky man and beating him and 'Slow Dancing Music', smooching with your girlfriend at the end of the night. One was called 'Standing at the Bus Stop', which was fast and gutsy. Even if Hannah wasn't my friend and sister, I would still really love her songs.

Our gang, that had now gone from seven to twelve, walked away after the gig; us sisters sang song after song from the band's repertoire. Course we had to do all the mad actions to make everyone laugh. 'I got the fever, I got the pool fever and I wanna keep playing all night.'

Some of us pretended we had pool cues in our hands and did cheesy over-the-top dancing, like we were in a crazy pool-playing musical. Without all the stalls and street theatre, Covent Garden shopping arena looked like it was an empty amphitheater. There was even a huge covered area that looked exactly like it was a stage. Once we spotted it that was it - you couldn't drag me off. It was so tempting to get up and go mad. That it wasn't just us wild sisters up there as some of the others in the gang got up as well. We carried on singing and dancing through the streets and into the bright lights of London's effervescent West End. The atmosphere was vibrant - taxis, cars, buses, people, all parading past us in this real-life, outdoor party. I wanted to dance and skip along forever.

Someone had invited us to a house party, so all we needed to do was get on a bus and head into the night. We managed to get onto the open platform at the back of a slow-moving bus, all except Hannah that is. The bus had started to speed up more and more as each one of us had climbed on board, and by the time she wanted to get on, it was moving too fast. Once we realized she wasn't there, we got hysterical laughing. Some of us stood on the platform and reached out to try and grab her hand so we could drag her on. She ran as fast as she could, trying not to give in to her laughter too much. The bus would slow down for us to nearly grab her, but then it would speed up again. We were screaming laughing, as our fingers just missed, touching again and again. 'Come on, come on,' we kept shouting to her.

All the people on the bus, who could see what was going on, were smiling and laughing at us.

With her face getting redder and her cheeks more and more puffed out, Hannah made one last big leap towards the bus and we finally managed to grab hold of her and yank her on board. We all cheered and roared with laughter, while the bus took us off into our perfect night.

Epilogue

By 1982 Cec had had enough of life in the Stepney squat, with its leaking roof and constant problems. Her relationship with her sister changed so Cec took the opportunity presented by a new friendship to move to Leytonstone, near Epping Forest in Essex. This was a complete change for her: she was no longer squatting but living in a house that was owned and occupied, with a four-poster bed and an Old English Sheepdog as well as indoor plumbing, a pool table and a Monkey Puzzle tree in the garden – a sign of middle-class sophistication in the late 1970s. Her friend had use of a convertible MG car at weekends, and Cec has fond memories of being chauffeured around the roads in the forest, whilst still travelling back to Manchester to see her Mam once a month.

From Leytonstone she moved back into London proper to a series of squats in Holloway, where the main women's prison in London is situated. Cec was closely involved with the South London Women's Centre in Brixton, acting as a bingo caller for social events. She also played friendly matches in a range of sports on Highbury Fields, turning out for Irish Women's teams for football (soccer), rounders and its near-cousin softball to play against teams for black women, working-class women and even middle-class women, all part of an extensive friendship group. Her dad commented that he was worried about her and warned, 'I don't know what you are doing but you are heading for prison'. Cec recalls that women criminals were regularly trying to recruit her to their gangs – her tough Mancunian upbringing gave some people the impression that she was less than entirely honest – but Dad's words steered her away from any temptation to stray from the narrow path. Cec eventually started working as a painter and decorator in North London, carrying cans of paint on the back of her bike and step ladders on buses.

Cec's political identity was continuing to develop. She has strong memories of a lesbian sex and sexuality conference where working-class women and women of color were silenced by middle-class women so in response they went outside and fundraised for a future working-class lesbian get-together. In 1983 that get-together happened in Leeds, West Yorkshire; there was a second event in 1984.

By 1985 Cec says she was less promiscuous, with just two girlfriends that year (though she was seeing both at the same time). Her journal records that she felt she was 'not giving way to my own needs in anything else but the high of hedonism'. In 1986 an Irish Women's Centre opened in Stoke Newington, and with it a new chapter opened. The full story follows in the next volume of the series...

20195202R00139

Printed in Great Britain
by Amazon